Amazed by Grace

BY *David A. Redding*

Amazed by Grace

David A. Redding

Fleming H. Revell Company
Old Tappan, New Jersey

Library of Congress Cataloging-in-Publication Data

Redding, David A.
    Amazed by grace.

    1. Grace (Theology)   2. Christian life—Presbyterian authors.   3. Redding, David A.   I. Title.
BT761.2.R43   1986   234   85-31189
ISBN 0-8007-1480-6

To the Glory of God
and to my sons and daughters
John and Jean
David and Bobbie
Mark and Sarah
and Marion

Contents

Acknowledgments

A book is written by many more people than those who get the praise or blame. Books live off the legacy of the language and previous books. The author is drawing upon all the things he was ever told, or experienced.

Increasingly I sense the gigantic debt to my father and mother, but my dear wife, Dee, and our children's blessed godmother, "Do," poured many improvements into this manuscript. My daughter, Marion, provided immeasurable editorial assistance.

Teachers who never knew they taught me, and angels I never knew were there, pop into my mind now and make me wonder how many more sources there actually are than I have quoted. All I know is that my pen is small compared to them. Yes, I still use a pen, lacking the fortitude and the eloquence demanded by a chisel.

I suppose this book's publication began with the overtime assistance of my secretary, Beth Walters Dixon, but my indebtedness extends to the officers and editors at Revell, who published my first five, and now my last two, books.

And now last, and perhaps most important of all, I make my final acknowledgment to you, my reader, the author's beloved "unknown soldier," without whom a book would never be written.

DAVID A. REDDING
SKY FARM

I

If It Isn't Amazing,
It Isn't Grace

However much we disagree about creation no one denies it was sensational. Everything God does is not only beautifully done, it is spectacular entertainment. He did not just create the universe, He dazzled earth with life by fantastic moves impossible to upstage.

I've read that Halley's comet, that tiny streak in the sky that reappears every seventy-six years, is three millions of miles long; and it is a cosmic trifle compared to the stupendous stars that God is spinning off the frontier of the universe at the moment. The astronomer Jeans guessed that there are already as many stars as there are grains of sand on all the seashores on Earth. You could dump several Earths into a crater on Jupiter.

We may not agree about how God did it, how long a day He put in those six or seven days, which even Scripture suggests could have been in years or eons. Was creation accomplished with "a big bang" or "a still small voice," or both, or better yet ... In Mark Twain's *Huckleberry Finn* as Huck Finn and Jim were drifting down the Mississippi on a raft at night, Huck said:

> We had the sky up there, all speckled with stars, and we used to lay on our backs and look up at them and discuss about whether they was made or only just happened. Jim, he allowed they was made, but I allowed they happened; I judged it would have took too long to make so many. Jim said the moon could 'a laid them; well, that looked kind of reasonable, so I didn't say nothing against it, cause I've seen a frog lay most as many, so of course it could be done. We used to watch the stars that fell, too, and see them streak down. Jim allowed they'd got spoiled and was hove out of the nest.

Whatever construction methods God used, coming up with a world like that was something else!

We can only wonder what it was like when earth broke away from the sun—certainly box office number one—and when the floods came that cooled it; or how it was when Australia surfaced, and when the flames of fire licked out of the sea and rained down Hawaii. But let us not permit our fussing over the sequence and the timing to distract us from being speechless and overawed: It was no "B" movie. Can't we all agree and bow the knee: "In the beginning God"?

Who's going to come up with a better way to begin and end the day than He does, day after day? Wherever you see the hand of God you see mind-boggling stars or a prairie sky on fire, snow that sweeps clean, each flake an original, or clouds and fog moving in to deepen the mystery. Kids aren't built from nuts and bolts, they're born like planets. And they don't just inflate into adulthood. Adolescence is as phenomenal as the change of seasons. Even our garden is not solely for eating; there's a blessed, blooming daisy, and we sing, "How Beautiful the Morning and the Day."

When the Queen of Sheba visited King Solomon, he apparently paraded everything he owned for her to review: elephants, horses, wives, and silver, I suppose, as far as the eye could see. In any event, she got so carried away by his magnificence that the Scripture reports: "There was no spirit left in her." Yet Jesus, standing in a relatively barren countryside pointed to a wild lily and declared, "Solomon in all his glory was not arrayed like one of these." The Creator of the heavens and the earth is not an "also ran." You'll never catch Him in some "ho hum."

God is not only amazing in nature, but also in His supernatural amazing grace. His re-creation of you and me is as spellbinding as earth's birthday. If we've been redeemed, and it was not one of those false pregnancies we pull on ourselves through some inane self-improvement program, we've undergone a transformation as awesome as God's installation of the solar system.

Many of us like to say that we oozed into Christianity without any fireworks; nothing happened to speak of. But if this be so, it cannot have been done by the electrifying finger of God that fired the sun. While we may not yet be aware of the drama, if it isn't amazing, it isn't grace.

Part of the reason we keep a low profile on any life-changing experience may be humility, although we're talking about *God's* grace aren't we? But the other reason may be those who have corrupted the idea of rebirth by grabbing the floor at every opportunity and dragging us through their smoothly simulated conversion about how they were saved at 3:30 A.M., November 10, when the floodwaters reached the third floor, and everything went black. There were shooting stars, a band of angels, and they suddenly lost their allergy to God, kids, and cats, and started being good ever since—though they don't explain why God apparently hung up on them way back when.

After repeatedly hearing these proud little bigots in ourselves, we do have an excuse for lying low over our encounter with God. But I want to question any smug assumption that Jesus Christ, Superstar, can ever touch anyone unmemorably. If God didn't celebrate your second birthday eventfully, I don't believe He had anything to do with it. Light can never swallow darkness anesthetically.

Some of the most tedious people in the world may insist that God has done them over. But their testimony is a little labored, and it gives *them* too much credit. They come off looking a little too good. God is not the convincingly creative hero of their contrived scenario. If our new lives are authentic, they will bear fruit in others, immediately detectable in laughter, and tears, and love.

Some of us shadowboxing Christians can almost bring off such manufacturing. Through sheer determination and painstaking sincerity we attend church incessantly, read the Bible religiously, run our legs off for God, even "give our bodies to be burned," but it doesn't catch fire; it doesn't take off. We have not received wings. Our heart has not yet been broken open. It is a forced cheer, and not a joy that spills out. Christ has not yet grafted us live onto Himself; we have tied ourselves onto Him as though we were a dried arrangement. We are too proud and too far gone to face how sterile and uncontagious we are. We have draped ourselves appropriately over God. He has not ecstatically re-created us.

This is precisely why Jesus picked Simon Peter for prominence. Because Peter fell into this very failing of counterfeiting Christianity. Peter was one of the first four disciples who began following Christ. He was the first to identify Christ. Jesus was free to use Peter's house, his boat, even his sword, the night Peter attended surgically to the soldier's ear. Peter ascended the mount of transfiguration and was in on scads of Christ's miracles. Peter was chosen for that ultimate prayer circle that Thursday night. Can you beat that? So Peter felt he had good reason to believe he was in like Flynn on the state of grace that signified redemption. And so he insisted that he was willing to go to the death, reassuring Jesus that he would never fail Him.

But Jesus tried to warn Peter that he was still his old self. The dam of disgrace had still not broken in Peter even late in that last week: "This night," Jesus told Peter, "before the rooster crows, you will deny Me three times" (Matthew 26:34). Peter was flabbergasted that he was not all set spiritually. But before that awful night was out, when his Lord needed him as never before, Peter had deserted Him in three sickening exposures, and the rooster was crowing furiously. Then, and not 'til then, did Peter at last look the Lord in the eye and go out and weep bitterly, and brokenly, and finally, thoroughly, into Christ Jesus.

Peter was no help at all in that second significant birth of his. After three years he was still a mess, still couldn't lift a finger in his own delivery. God had to do him completely over. Peter had nothing to boast of, everything to repent of, and what happened to him was as brilliant and as solo a move on God's part as to bring up the sun in a black sky, or in you and me.

Mark Twain, in his autobiography, recalled the way watermelon entertained a boy's insides. The Bread of Heaven also enthralls the mind and soul of man. It is "sweeter than honey." The wine that Christ made from water at Cana was the best, the most expensive. How could such a God answer any prayer without bringing down the house?

That was back in Bible times, but it must happen now to the most perfect churchman from Missouri. He's no better than the old Simon Peter until he too is taken apart and put back together again as only God can do. A mass a day won't do it, nor a neat little prayer time, nor seminary. Only the One who is "the way, the truth, and the life," can midwife you and me back to life again for good.

It happens all the time in Alcoholics Anonymous. None of those drunks, as they call themselves, are ever saved in some routine group plan. It is always one by one, each incredible and unique. I have known so many dramatically restored addicts, who a day at a time demonstrate this unpretentious biblical miracle. No doubt remains in my mind but that the Creator continues to add fresh stars to His spiritual firmament as astronomically as out in distant space itself.

I have never sat through "a pitch" in AA that wasn't absorbing. When I hear from one of those vermin-ridden saints who went to hell and back I cry my eyes out and laugh 'til my sides ache, so penetrating is God's theatre—not man's put-up job. The phonies in AA are policed by intoxication. They can't get away with the deceit that diseases the church.

The secret of the eloquence of a member of Alcoholics Anonymous is not Public Speaking 301; it is that endangered virtue, honesty. The speaker at such a meeting is commissioned to stand up and speak, not as an authority, but as a victim. He makes a fool of himself for God. He tells the futile, funny story of his own comic-tragic heartbreak: How God had to go all the way to come and find him in the most embarrassing position, when he had not a shred of self-respect left. And this combination of someone's utter humility and the love of God that will stop at nothing has the most redemptive and sustaining effect on all the listeners. The pointing finger and harsh voice of the pulpit is the opposite of "How Sweet the Sound."

It isn't just liquor or drugs that these addicts are saved from. What's really at issue is our being proud as Lucifer. Our fatal enemy is pride, and it is our pride by which we all are mortally wounded, whether our symptom is a chemical dependence or a more cleverly concealed symptom, such as infects many of us down front in church.

One alcoholic I knew stopped drinking, but became so unbearable and grandiose an egomaniac that his wife spiked his orange juice with vodka. He had only become a "dry drunk." Sobriety doesn't save you, although sobriety usually requires the blasting of our pride that every one of us needs, drunk or sober.

A physician was sitting to my left in a circle of friends one summer at Laity Lodge, that beloved conference ground offered to us all by the Howard E. Butt Foundation, of Kerrville, Texas. This distinguished man possessed such a sweet spirit of humility I finally found myself exclaiming, "Didn't you say you were a doctor?" And he said, "Yes," and I replied, "Well, why aren't you acting like Almighty God?" And in a way that moved me closer to him, he replied, "I'm a drunk."

Preachers too can be proud as Caiaphas. Recently a Presbyterian Congress of Renewal was held in Dallas. I was told it was the largest gathering of Presbyterians ever. What would renew us? Our hope was obscured by that word, *renewal.* That word was not strong enough and revealed our pride, which is at the bottom of our problem. The fatal poison that has been shrinking the church so rapidly in recent years, and rendering it as fruitless as a spiritual desert, is our pride—our pride, for instance, in thinking that drunks need to be saved but that the rest of us "good people" only need to be "renewed."

This pride was perhaps reflected, in a sermon when a preacher boasted he had been married to the same wife as though for 300 years; no matter how long he said it was, it certainly upstaged a great number in the audience who had been separated or divorced. And such a statement hardly elevated following speakers under fire for their divorces. Since my first wife still suffers me as her husband perhaps I'll take the liberty of saying that "all have sinned." "We have turned every one, to his own way" (Isaiah 53:6).

While we do not condone divorce or drunkenness, we recognize that our own pride is far worse. And I believe that Saint Peter himself would insist that what he did, which illustrates what we all are and do in one way or another, is far worse than the public sins to which we can point or condescend. It is as though we were dead ringers for the proud Pharisee crying loud the prayer Christ said God never heard: "God, I thank you that I am not like other men—extortioners, unjust, adulterers, or even as this tax collector" (Luke 18:11).

Another of our distinguished clergy inadvertently approached the edge of the breakthrough we're all dying for. He reported that a madman solemnly invaded one of his church services and shouted to the preacher in a commanding voice: "God sent me to tell you to repent of your pride." The preacher defended himself, naturally, just as I would have tried to do, hastily reassuring his audience, not only that he was equal to the situation, but also in solid on this basic Christian prerequisite.

However, this *is* the very place where we're all stuck and continue to fool ourselves as did Simon Peter: "Lord, we are ready . . . you know." No. Soon the cock will crow on us clergy, elders, cardinals, bumper-sticker, lapel-labeled disciples. Fools, children, and clowns are not afraid to tell the truth; God prompted that disturbed man in church to tell on us all.

Everyone needs to fall down in front of that disreputable prophecy and admit it. We should never get up from that hard floor until our pride is repented, not simply in words in some church service, but so fruitfully that when we got up the world would rise with us. And the awakening at last come that will never come until we come back and finish the work on the original mission field, ourselves—which is still holding up everything.

When I ministered at Flagler Presbyterian Church in St. Augustine, we used to observe Maundy Thursday Communion at night in silence. The choir sang the Scripture of Holy Week, and the old curator limped down the aisle of that beautiful "Cathedral of North Florida" carrying a full-size crossbeam, which he then would spike in place, the hammer blows echoing in the darkened candlelight. He would then hang a crown of thorns on the cross.

The first night we performed this service, there could not have been many present in that cavernous place. The failure of the crowd could have been due to my inadequate publicity, or ministry for that matter, but as any minister would understand, I was deeply disappointed. As we went through that service, which was silent except for the music and the sounds associated with Calvary—such as the counting out of the thirty pieces of silver and hearing their ringing on the marble floor—I kept hearing the sound of a man somewhere in the church sobbing uncontrollably. I doubt if I could have borne being any nearer to the Cross that night than that weeping brought me: To me it must have been like that when Simon Peter finally fell off his spiritual perch, and at last perceived "Christ looking at him" and "went out and wept bitterly."

Something like that unforgettable Thursday night, that brought that man from his dark old world into an incandescent ministry, is in store for all of us. Not until then will Christ come back again and we be able, finally, in the words of the spiritual, "to walk in Jerusalem just like John."

2

*Except for a Miracle
the World Is Lost*

It was only a century ago that we were engaged in a great Civil War testing, as Lincoln wrote in his Gettysburg Address, whether this nation, or any other nation could long endure. Now our world is split by a curtain of iron, and each night folks shiver in bed wondering if they'll make the morning before everything goes up in the smoke of a mushroom cloud.

Every conceivable plan of military preparedness and peace by diplomacy is being attempted as we plunge deeper into an abyss bristling with nuclear warheads and barrels of fire and brimstone warnings pounded out on tables at the United Nations. The 40,000 American boys who died that dreadful day at the Battle of Antietam seems old hat now to the imminent massacre of an Armageddon.

Shuffling tyrants in the Kremlin won't help. And while we don't know what else to do but bankrupt ourselves by skyrocketing defense against a bully, in the end the most brilliant "star wars" defense system is no doubt doomed. But in the meantime we can also default.

Phúc, a Vietnamese boat person who came to live with us, had been a sophomore at the University of Saigon. We could hear her sobbing through the bedroom wall at night over the letters she received from her broken family battling the fury of the Communists to whom we had deserted them.

Phúc was born in Hanoi as the Iron Curtain was cutting off North Vietnam. Her noble-born mother was so traumatized by the calamity she could never after remember Phúc's birthday any closer than late that summer. Phúc's father was a colonel on duty back at their family home in Saigon, which was where all four grandparents still lived. Then a high Communist official fell in love with Phúc's mother, and not knowing what else to do she agreed to marry him if in return he would fly her children to their father in Saigon. He agreed, but at the last minute she also slipped aboard the plane. But, as we know, that sweet reunion was very temporary and soon Saigon too fell and Phúc was forced to face the slim chance of the "boat persons." They were reduced to drinking the urine of the babies when they were finally picked up by an Israeli ship.

Americans felt so relieved to abandon Vietnam, but leaving our vulnerable friends over there was nothing to be proud of. Just because Vietnam is not as much in the news now doesn't mean we settled it, or that Communism isn't hastening from there to further encircle the globe. The Bolsheviks only began in Russia in World War I. Now look: China, Yugoslavia, North Korea, Vietnam, Hungary. It's as close as Cuba. Central America? God help Africa.

Aleksandr Solzhenitsyn says that the Communists thought of everything in their atheistic scheme to pave the world. They forgot nothing, except one thing: a miracle. Is the world itself like a drunken man who will stop at nothing, until he hits the floor and finally looks to God for help? In these last desperate hours of the twentieth century, that is the hope I am beginning to see. Without more amazing grace, we're gone.

Solzhenitsyn, a Russian captain at the German front in World War II, made a slurring remark about Stalin in a letter to a friend. It was caught by the censors and reported to the NKVD, who arrested the captain and flung him into one of the chain of Soviet labor camps. These camps, which comprise an area larger than the Republic of France, he named the Gulag Archipelago.

Solzhenitsyn was buried alive in these concentration camps for eight years. He has described *One Day in the Life* . . . of such a prisoner. It was worse than the life of rats and cannibals. Even the improved prison, reserved for mathematicians and scientists such as he, which he enjoyed for a while, was still only *The First Circle* of Dante's hell, as he was later to write it to the world.

But in the midst of this inferno, this miracle by which I believe God is going to work everything out far better began to take shape. And I pray it comes before the necessity of another and bloodier Gettysburg.

While he suffered this prison, Solzhenitsyn's wife divorced him. Both his parents had died. As he reached the end of his eight-year sentence, he came down with a cancer in his abdomen so virulent that each night he could tell it had grown that day. It was then, in that utter desolation and darkness, that the Light of the World shone so brightly upon him. Here are the crucial sentences of the prayer that came to him following that black hour. I believe it is the prayer that only comes when one has despaired of every other possible solution:

> O Lord, how easy to believe in You . . . I am
> astonished by the path through despair you
> have provided me. . . .

After all hope had gone, it was then God came, utterly filling with joy that vast excavation suffering had made. Salvation came to this victim of the Soviet Bear without the assistance of any Sunday school teacher or missionary from the West. God came, as Job found, after everything else had gone: "I have heard of You by the hearing of the ear, But now my eye sees You" (Job 42:5). Was this a miniature rehearsal of the way God intends to photo finish all earth itself?

The incredible saga of Solzhenitsyn's redemption has been pouring out upon us in an unparalleled flood of books. For the first time the truth has been told on the bullies in the Communist hierarchy—not only on Stalin but the horror story of atrocities and crimes that have bathed Russia in the blood of a hundred million, many of them unsung martyrs of the faith. Three huge volumes of *The Gulag Archipelago,* in how many languages, cover the planet in an incredible literary achievement.

Solzhenitsyn's *The Oak and the Calf* chronicles his story of writing in prison without pencil and paper. In the writing class I presume to teach each June at Laity Lodge near Kerrville, Texas, I tell my students to do their writing, as I am doing now, on a yellow tablet, and daily at a familiar desk. Solzhenitsyn had no desk, no utensils, not even time to write, for he was forced to squander all his daylight at hard labor. So, like the tribal storyteller in Africa, he wrote volumes in his head, setting his sentences to meter, spending one week each month committing to memory what he'd written in his head while working as a mason with his hands.

When Solzhenitsyn was finally freed from prison

and exiled in Russia, he still had to outwit the heavy censorship imposed by Big Brother, so he wrote all he had memorized on onionskin in a tiny minuscule script, and rolled up the sheets in wine bottles and buried them in the garden. From there he spirited them to the free world, but they also circulate in Russia by *Samizdat,* which is the word for the underground method of publishing by which each reader hand copies one for another.

Is it not an arresting phenomenon that this great writer of modern times, who now lives in Vermont, comes from Russia? Malcolm Muggeridge believes that Solzhenitsyn and Mother Teresa of Calcutta are two angels God has spirited to us in these critical hours, neither of whom was born and bred in the land of the free and the home of the brave.

How can this be? The few Bibles the Communists publish are only to fool naive visitors into thinking that religious freedom exists behind the Iron Curtain. Nothing could be further from the truth. Aside from the "officially permitted" churches, those who attend the severely restricted churches that do exist are shadowed and harassed by the KGB, although this is always done under the pretext of the church members' having committed other supposed infractions.

Solzhenitsyn can only be explained by the discipleship of Tolstoy, a great Christian writer in Russia who lived at the turn of the century. Stalin censored all Christian writings when he came to power, but not

Tolstoy's, as Malcolm Muggeridge learned firsthand
and reported to us in *The End of Christendom* (Wm.
B. Eerdmans, 1980):

> Anatoli Kusnyetsov, the Soviet writer whom I
> interviewed, said, when asked how it was
> that he had this Christian orientation, that
> Stalin made one fatal error: he neglected to
> suppress the works of Tolstoy. Again I detect
> a miracle. If you scoured the literature of the
> centuries of Christendom for the books that
> might most help an oppressed people in rela-
> tion to our Lord and the Christian faith, you
> could find nothing better than the short
> stories and the later novels of Tolstoy. The
> efforts of Radio Free Europe, radio liberation,
> the Voice of America, and the overseas ser-
> vice of the BBC, all put together, wouldn't
> equal one single short story of Tolstoy in
> keeping alive in the hearts of human beings
> the knowledge of the love of God.

Tolstoy's writings are filled with passages from the
Gospels. This stupendous miracle is already cracking
the atheistic Communist indoctrination of the world.
For not only Solzhenitsyn, but multitudes of others in
Russia, are being deeply moved by this giant saint.
Many couples continue to be married on Tolstoy's
grave.

No greater example of Christian writing exists than Tolstoy's *War and Peace*. All of Stalin's brutal efforts have not succeeded in suppressing such evangelical keepsakes as this story of Tolstoy's (*Russian Stories and Legends,* Pantheon Books) that I retell briefly here:

An honest and hardworking Russian peasant, named Aksenov left his dear wife and family for a few days to visit a nearby fair. He spent his first overnight at an inn during which a murder was committed. The murderer placed the murder weapon in the sleeping peasant's bag. The police discovered him that way in the morning. He was stuck in prison for twenty-six years, surviving on bitter hopes of revenge. One day the real murderer was imprisoned with him and soon charged with an escape attempt. He had been digging a tunnel that Aksenov alone had witnessed. The authorities interrogated the peasant about this crime, granting him at long last his opportunity for revenge, for on the peasant's word his enemy would be flogged almost to death.

Aksenov was asked to bear witness to the crime, and as only Tolstoy can tell the story, instead of jumping at the chance, the grace of God suddenly wells up in the peasant's heart, and he finds the darkness in him has fled, and he is filled with light. He finds himself saying to the officers: "I saw nothing."

That night the guilty criminal makes his way to the

peasant's bunk and, sobbing on his knees, begs his forgiveness. And again the light of Christ floods the peasant's heart. "God will forgive you," said he. "Maybe I am a hundred times worse than you." And at these words his heart grew light and the longing for home left him. He no longer had any desire to leave the prison. The joy of forgiveness far surpassed the luxury of freedom itself.

Is it not astonishing that, in addition to *Samizdat* and smuggled Bibles, the writings of such a powerful exponent of the Gospel are allowed to circulate behind the Iron Curtain today?

This is no time to give up praying for Russia. Malcolm Muggeridge insists that there are more true Christians behind the Iron Curtain than in the free world, for no one fakes it there, for fear of reprisal. One risks one's life and reputation to confess Christ. No one dares Christianity unless he means it, but how can he not dare when the sinister, atheistic propaganda is subjected to so bright a light as Tolstoy still shines upon it?

The leaven of Christ's Kingdom continues to work from Tolstoy through Solzhenitsyn in many ways I am not aware of, but let me share one way. In Zurich after Solzhenitsyn was exiled from Russia in 1974, he established the Russian Social Fund from his royalties to care for the forsaken families of political prisoners in Russia. Such prisoners have been incarcerated on some trumped-up charge, but actually because of their religious faith, or because they spoke out on behalf of freedom and individual rights. No mercy is shown to their wives and children left behind. The wives' reputations are ruined, so they cannot find or keep any jobs. Solzhenitsyn's social fund was set up to save these victims, and aid prisoners after their release. Imagine how hostile the Communists would be to such an embarrassing exposure of their heartlessness.

The wonder of this social fund was that it reached out and touched my life too. The most famous custodian of this fund was a man named Alexander Ginzburg, who had formerly been a journalist and secretary of André Sakharov, the physicist and Nobel peace prize winner, perhaps best known of all Russian dissidents as a spokesman for world peace.

Thousands of rubles were distributed by the brave and compassionate Ginzburg before he was imprisoned. He kept the list of his charities in his head to protect them. He could be awakened at night and recall the names of those most in need of his next dispensation. His battle for freedom and human kindness accumulated three devastating prison terms at hard labor, finally in a glass factory that jeopardized his frail health. When his fiancée, Irina, visited the prison to be married to him, he gestured to his fellow prisoners sitting in the bleak visiting area: "You should know that I must give them all my strength."

The Solzhenitsyns organized a committee in the

United States to free Alexander Ginzburg. I found myself the only minister on it and wrote letters in his behalf and encouraged others in our country to do so. Apparently there *were* others and soon we were seeing by the news that President Carter was exchanging two Soviet spies for five Russian dissidents, including Alexander Ginzburg.

Out of thanks for the tiny part I played in his freedom, he visited my farm home and later Laity Lodge in Texas to confer on my friends and me a two-week stay that will remain one of the wonders of our lives.

It was only too obvious that he had been beaten and sickened by his harsh imprisonments, but when questioned he would brush it away with, "No, the hard part was the screams of the others." And when pushed, he would answer in halting English, "I have the gift . . . to be a prisoner." We had been talking about our "gifts" at Laity Lodge, but the gift of martyrdom had not occurred to any of the rest of us.

We enjoyed two Creativity Weeks with him that summer at Laity Lodge. Classes by skilled master craftsmen were held in such fields as blacksmithing, silver, pottery, oil, and watercolors. I wondered how our spartan Russian could endure our Madison Avenue mentality in that lovely setting in the hill country along the Frio River. It seemed to me that the most difficult thing for him to accept might be the preoccupation with tennis of almost all of us there.

At first he hung back from entering the courts. Finally we realized it was because of the forbidding fence that to him must have been a chilling reminder. But he entered on his second day and soon shared the adulation we all felt for our beloved tennis coach. Ginzburg made gifts for the many friends he had made, but his first prize, a full-size copper enameled tennis ball, went to the coach, in a wholehearted acceptance of our way of life, and the greatness he perceived in Henry Parish.

When our visit with this hero of the free world ended, he paid the folks of Laity Lodge the ultimate compliment. He said, "You are the most wonderful people I've ever met, except for convicts."

The miracle that will save the world will enlist us. Christians must learn from convicts how to die rather than give up their faith in a God who is both "the author and the finisher of our faith."

3.

Beauty Will
Save the World

An amazing amount of grace existed before language, and its tongue was beauty. Before there were words, savages saw and treasured beautiful things. There were pictures on the wall of the cave before there were names and initials. And they prayed back then by sunrise and starlight, and by the beauty in each other's eyes long before they had a book to go by. It is still so. As Solzhenitsyn said in his Nobel Prize address:

Art warms even an icy and depressed heart, opening it to lofty spiritual experience. By means of art we are sometimes sent—dimly,

brief—revelations unattainable by reason.
Like that little mirror in the fairy tales—look
into it, and you will see not yourself but, for a
moment, that which passeth understanding,
a realm to which no man can ride or fly. And
for which the soul begins to ache.

The title of this chapter, "Beauty Will Save the
World," is from Dostoevski, and I have been busy discovering that beauty's converts are legion. Beauty may
be the only language that can escape the perversion of
the propagandist, and leap over the barriers that tear
our world apart.

Of course we believe that Christ is the Saviour of
the world, but it was "in the beauty of the lilies Christ
was born across the sea"; and in the most majestic and
glorious pageantry that ever took place upon the earth,
He was born under the star to the anthems of angels.
His ministry was a parade of wonders and His parables
literary gems, opening wide the gates of Jerusalem on
that glorious Palm Sunday. He died and came back
from the dead, in a stunning rehearsal of the climax to
the hopes of all the world.

The Gospel is not simply good news. It is a master-
piece, and *its beauty will save the world.*

You cannot catch Christ boring or ugly. If it isn't
amazing, it isn't grace, and if it isn't beautiful, it isn't
Gospel. As the old hymn goes: "Wonderful Words,
Beautiful Words, Wonderful Words of Life."

The action of grace is never bad mannered or defensive. We'll never convince anyone, really, with our hands upon his lapel, backing him into a corner. We will not change someone's life by honking because we say we love Jesus, by bumper stickers, or by a clutter of road signs, or fluttering tracts. Evangelism is a much more demanding art than a busload of frantic believers barging in uninvited on unsuspecting sunbathers along a beach in Florida.

So many forms of help are born of desperation and are essentially negative, achieving slim legislative gains, but never the required ground swell. Such noisy rallies as Carry Nation's hatchet crusade against the saloons, or the vigilantes' malpractice of lynchings, or even many other more reputable marches on behalf of some worthy cause, lack imagination and distract each of us from our more fruitful Christian vocations. Such mass movements excuse us from the tremendous influence we can have on others in our daily lives by such artistry as Mother Teresa exemplifies.

Jesus, not only in His Beatitudes, but in His entire ministry, even to His entry into Jerusalem, brought a contagious atmosphere of joy, never resorting to manipulative pressure. Most of His life was dedicated to a heart-to-heart transformation, one on one. This approach now, even in world literacy, as Frank Laubach taught, "Each one teach one," is still so superior a way to win the world for anything. Working up the masses, and coercing people with superficial messages and simplistic slogans, is generally antagonistic and ultimately futile. Even its temporary gains incite too much antagonism. Only beauty "will save the world."

We save the world as well as each other by love, and love doesn't pull a fast one, or put something over on someone. Love doesn't simply go by the book: It takes nothing less than friendship. Love is in no hurry, and "does not behave rudely" (*see* 1 Corinthians 13). Love moves when the time is right. Love knows how to wait, how to listen, how to be loved. Love allows surprises. Love is lovely. War is ugly, but "there is no beauty that we should desire him" (Isaiah 53:2 KJV).

A few years ago Laity Lodge inaugurated the week of creativity I have mentioned, in addition to their usual weeks of study and reflection. A hasty kibitzer might have dismissed the idea as a little presumptuous, because only God is creative. Or that grown-ups were simply going back to summer Vacation Bible School, with its emphasis on crafts and the outdoors. But that would have overlooked our concept of rescuing Christianity from its hard chairs; we wanted to rise above the idea that all Christians ever did was sit and toss around a few ideas.

One can learn about God without words. We chose to see God in the beautiful things we made together under the eye of a master silversmith, to find Him through music as well as lectures, through drama, and not only in memory verses. I have already referred to Alexander Ginzburg's participation in two Creativity Weeks, but I want now to share some of the creations of the students in what was nicknamed the Little Redding Writing Class.

At a religious conference we usually think of getting into "the Word" in an evangelist's scintillating Bible study, a superior religious exercise that I do not disparage. However, we must never sink to so provincial and unimaginative a view as to assume that prayer and Bible study, with a little music and charity thrown in, exhausts all religious activities. Just about everything, even with all the delays, finally leads to God, either to His courtroom or His throne room. Let me share the avenue that leads to Him through the art of writing.

The art of writing is not confined to a few; it is the unrecognized talent of everyone who can sign checks. Beauty will save the world. I've seen it rescue worlds in my writing class. The Word of God itself often gives rise to the words in someone's head that need to be put down and said before one is read into the Kingdom.

I remember one dear little grandmotherly woman who enrolled in my writing class with an apology for ever leaving the kitchen stove and inflicting so illiterate a pupil upon me. I took her word for it and listened to the "deathless prose" of the others while she sat in humble silence at our feet. On the last day of class I asked if she had a contribution. Robert Frost said that writing is making connections, and we had featured the point that week, illustrating it from the parables that master that art; for instance, how Jesus related leaven to the way His Kingdom works.

My little grandmother surprised me. She explained first that a mongrel dog had adopted her family. They named the dog Brandon, and since she took care of him, Brandon followed her everywhere with adoring eyes. Her line was a keeper: "O Lord, when You come to judge me, please look at me through Brandon's eyes."

Not only can everyone write, everyone is the only authority on, for instance, the lump in his or her throat. And writing about one's suffering economizes words and produces eloquence. Basic to our literacy is not simply English 101, but brutal frankness about our deepest feelings. Solzhenitsyn says that it is his suffering that wins his readers' attention; suffering sifts truth to the surface like nothing else.

Our first assignment in the writing class is to write three epitaphs: your father's, your mother's, and your own. I am continually astonished by the dramatic literary power that explodes from those agonizing secrets that practically strike us inarticulate. Psychiatrists are not the only ones who recognize the priority of facing our first idols, or demons. I have often seen these feelings rupture with such incredibly memorable lines. The frightening beauty of looking at our life before our guard is up will help save the world, not only our little world.

Sitting in a circle, always in the same seating order, I turned to my left and invited a woman to share the epitaph she had written for her father. She exclaimed, "Oh, we did that last year." We continued 'til halfway round, when that same woman began to weep and asked if she could be forgiven for her discourtesy, and have her turn back. She said: "Listening to you all has somehow opened my grief for the first time, and my father's epitaph has just come to comfort me. I must explain first that my father broke horses for a living, and when he died, I was the one who found him in the bathroom. The epitaph that just now burst upon me is: "He broke horses, and sometimes he was thrown."

What is the line that comes to you when you think of your father? One woman replied: "I'd rather wait in the car." Another said: "He was always right." Other students buried their folks together. "They tried to smell the roses"; "Will the controversy never end"; "Their legacy was hatred." For my own folks I wrote: "The flames from the ruins of their lives illumined heaven for me." One wrote of her mother: "She said she was not afraid."

Epitaphs for ourselves can be funny. W. C. Fields' was supposed to be: "On the whole, I'd rather be in Philadelphia." And that of a well-known hypochondriac: "I told you I was sick." Two of my students were not prepared, so one said: "I pass," and the other: "I did not hear the assignment," both of which made good epitaphs. Malcolm Muggeridge, former editor of *Punch*, said that the most beautiful line to him, and one that would serve well as an epitaph, was in *King Lear*. After Gloucester had been blinded he said: "I stumbled when I saw."

Beauty saving the world is like this: A father enrolled in our writing class. He had been in the oil fields, and did not consider himself literate, but he said that he needed to write a long overdue letter to his estranged twenty-four-year-old son, a copy of which he said he had also mailed to him that day. When his turn came, he read brokenly and with all his heart this letter:

My Dear Son,

Oh, how I long to be with you. Now it is too late to have you present as an infant or young child. When you were growing up I was away from home earning money to feed and clothe your body, not taking time to feed your soul. May the good Lord help to convey to you, now that you are an adult, my yearning for you to be joyful and peaceful. May He give me strength and knowledge to somehow let you know that you are accepted by me, that I love you as you are. May He take away the scars you carry from never being able to perform capably in my sight, and thereby release you to attain a greater sense of self-worth. I am sorry for criticizing everything you did or said. I failed to encourage or compliment you in your endeavors. For this I am truly sad. May our meetings from this day forward have the ingredient of praise flowing from me to you. May God give me courage to tell you of your goodness.

I now know it is because of you that I have come to know the Saviour, Jesus Christ. Only because of problems between us a few years ago did it become possible for me to understand that there is Someone greater and stronger and more powerful than me. Had it not been for you, I would never have turned to the Lord. For this I shall be ever grateful.

You have made it possible for me to accept you and many others as all of you are, without trying to change or correct you. I no longer get uptight just because someone does differently than I want. Had it not been for you I would still be trying to direct everyone in my whole world, and being miserable from it. You have been forgiven for everything that you might think I hold against you, but I have never told you this. Please know and believe this as it comes from my heart. And son, please find it in your heart to

forgive me for all the wrongs I have committed against you. If possible, may we start
anew. Thank God for sending you, and his
Son into my life through you.

Your loving father,

As you can imagine, this letter blew the writing
class away to God. It was not the most elegant prose,
but it had the rugged beauty of deep honesty and the
power of a life-changing experience. I asked that father if I could read his letter to the whole assembly on
our final evening together. He agreed so long as it
would be anonymous.

That assembly included another estranged father
and son. That son knew his father had also been a
member of the writing class. The mother had somehow gotten the two of them to come to that week together. During my reading of that letter that night,
this son elbowed his father and said: "Dad, you wrote
that letter to me, didn't you?" And the father, who had
not written the letter, nodded, and for the first time in
many years, they put their arms around each other.

Both those sons were reconciled to their fathers by
that one letter. The son to whom the letter was addressed is now in business with his father, and the
other son responded: "All is forgiven."

Such beauty will save the world. The police can't
save it, nor the fear a belligerent evangelizer arouses to
move people down the sawdust trail, nor fanatic road-

signs, nor loads of good works, not even giving our body to be burned. Beauty will save the world. "O Lord, our God, how excellent is thy name in all the earth" (Psalms 8:9 KJV).

Christ defended the beautiful thing a woman did to him against Judas' condemnation that the gift should have been spent on the poor: "Mary took a whole pint of very expensive perfume made of nard, poured it on Jesus' feet, and wiped them with her hair . . . until its fragrance filled the house" (*see* John 12:3).

The blessing for which even the poor languish will not be accomplished simply by saving them from starvation. They too will be saved only by beauty. It is not food, nor some fair share for which all the world is dying, but for the fragrance that can fill the house.

This fragrance, or beauty, is what is perfectly fascinating for us—what we were made to see, what our spirits long for, the bread of heaven.

I suppose the truly beautiful is the face of God, which we see only in snatches through a glass darkly, in the falling autumn leaves, the sun setting behind the sycamores, or hear in the laughter of the children playing in the apple tree.

Beauty to me is that penitent father's letter sobbed out to his son, or that grief-stricken daughter, for the first time finding the beauty of her father lying there in that grim bathroom.

I have seen beautiful things: someone who has suffered enough, someone who has sacrificed what she wanted more than anything else for someone else— like the woman bathing the feet of Christ in dear perfume.

Someone made that fiendish contraption of the cross into the most beautiful thing on earth. Do we not most reflect His beauty when we glory in it? This is the beauty that enthralls the soul: "Jesus keep me near the Cross. . . . Bring its scenes before me."

4

*Amazing Grace
Is a "Him"*

"Amazing Grace" is a hymn that came literally out of the slave traffic in the 1700s. John Newton, the author of what has become "the American hymn," confessed that he had been a militant atheist and deeply involved in that filthy business of man's inhumanity to man.

Newton was born in 1725, lost his mother to consumption when he was seven, and at eleven went to sea to serve on the ship commanded by his terrifying father. He was impressed into the British navy at eighteen, stripped and flogged for desertion, but survived and in two years broke away to enlist on a slaver running blacks from Africa to Charleston, South Carolina. According to one account Newton became so despicable a wretch that when he was washed overboard in a storm, his shipmates harpooned him in the leg rather than rescue him humanely.

At twenty-three, while he was at the helm, they sailed into a storm of such fury it appeared that the ship would go down, certainly dooming the cargo full of slaves locked in the hold below. That crisis turned Newton right-side up, and he gave his life to God.

Newton finally obtained orders to become an Anglican priest and wrote many hymns, including "Amazing Grace," which came out of his deliverance that awful night at sea. The epitaph he wrote for himself confesses the same story: "John Newton . . . appointed to preach the faith he had long laboured to destroy."

Authorities in American hymnology don't shed much light on the tune to which "Amazing Grace" is usually sung. Hymnals credit it as being an early American melody. It is said to have come from the rural South some time before the War Between the States, perhaps from Appalachia. In whomever's heart it was born, that haunting melody has in the last few years become the all-time American favorite. I never realized how beautiful it was until the following event, which fittingly introduced it to me.

Shortly after I moved to St. Augustine to be minister of Flagler Presbyterian Church, it was evident that the old Roosevelt pipe organ was ruined by age, neglect, or perhaps by climate. In any event, I phoned H. M. and Tressa Johnson to inquire if I could drive the ten miles down to Summer Haven to talk with them about something preposterous: "Please do, Mr. Redding," she said, "H. M. and I like to talk about preposterous things." The Johnsons had told me on my arrival in St. Augustine to let them know if I ever needed them. I did, then.

H. M. had made out Andrew Mellon's first income tax return. At ninety he still possessed the sparkle, wit, and trustworthiness that led Mellon to put all his property temporarily in H. M. Johnson's name.

I informed the Johnsons that we had been told that our pipe organ was in ruins and that I had consulted with the Aeolian-Skinner Organ Company in Boston, the most respected organ builders at that time. They had informed me that it would require $125,000 to begin to undertake the construction of a pipe organ of sufficient rank suitable for such a magnificent church—a church that was probably visited by as many tourists as any other in North America.

After our conference Mrs. Johnson said, "Mr. Redding, we'll call you within an hour." They did. The only difficulty was that they both wanted to use their own separate funds to give the new pipe organ.

It was just about the last Aeolian-Skinner pipe organ built before the company's tragic bankruptcy. And while it was not an excessively large bequest, even then, the Johnsons were not all that wealthy. Yet they had swiftly responded to our need at a time of advanced age when most people, even of means, would have been tempted to prudently preserve what legacy they had.

Tressa Johnson finally won out in the contest between the two of them as to who would give the organ,
and to this day, when I think of her and the beautiful
fruit her gift of music has already brought to so many,
I think again of Mary, who bathed the feet of Christ in
expensive perfume, "until its fragrance filled the
house."

When the time came to dedicate that magnificent
instrument, we obtained the services of the distinguished organist of Saint John the Divine in New York
City, a vast cathedral significant to me because of its
continuing construction across generations; and also
because my graduation exercises from midshipman's
school at Columbia University during World War II
were held there.

The dedicatory concert that Sunday afternoon built
up to a crescendo that shook the building. Huge
speakers which had been set in the aisles broadcast, as
well, such sounds as the takeoff of a 747 jet.

Immediately after the cacophony of this deafening
music, the organist emerged from behind the mahog-
any screen that concealed the bench to announce that
he would now play the gospel melody that was to
America what the tune "Greensleeves" was to
England. With one finger he played "Amazing Grace."
I love that song in many arrangements, but it has
never moved me more than that one-finger arrangement after such a nerve-shattering prelude.

There must be volumes that could be written about

"our song." It has been sung by individuals as diverse as John Wayne and Anita Bryant, and arranged for bagpipes and with Bach, but I must mention my friend, Colonel Dick Lockhart. He went with Admiral Richard Byrd on his last expedition to Antarctica. This military frontier in the forties was surrounded with the kind of charisma that we have experienced more recently over the moon landings. Dick shared his experience with us one evening during Lent at Liberty Church:

> I was an officer on that expedition and fully shared the spirit of adventure on that historic voyage, which heightened as we sailed into those frigid uncharted waters.
>
> Suddenly a wall of ice twelve-hundred feet high loomed beside us as far as the eye could see. Everyone on board came on deck, speechless and spellbound. The chaplain started softly singing "Amazing Grace" and the crew joined in, kneeling one by one. I remained standing until the third verse, then I too kneeled down and met Christ.

Amazing Grace

Amazing grace! how sweet the sound
That saved a wretch like me!
I once was lost, but now am found,
Was blind, but now I see.

'Twas grace that taught my heart to fear
And grace my fears relieved;
How precious did that grace appear
The hour I first believed!

Through many dangers, toils and snares,
I have already come;
'Tis grace has brought me safe thus far,
And grace will lead me home.

The Lord has promised good to me,
His word my hope secures;
He will my shield and portion be
As long as life endures.

When we've been there ten thousand years,
Bright shining as the sun,
We've no less days to sing God's praise
Than when we'd first begun.

This hymn touches our hearts so poignantly in this country because, despite our fierce pride, something deep within us identifies with that brokenhearted slaver, John Newton, and responds to the offer of pardon as he did.

That hymn happened to all of us too, in some way, on the way over to America, for America has had more slaves than anybody else. We, too, were runaways from old European families, rebelling like shameless prodigals from the very proper old country, killing each other off by the hundreds of thousands in the most bitter family feud any country ever had. And now even the most respectable Bostonian can see himself out on the plains in our cowboy myth, standing beside his horse, with his Stetson and his heart in his hand, singing with a western twang this old gospel song: "Amazing Grace."

We are trained on earth to work to win the trophies of success. We are ambitious to get both the credit and the control. A good person to us is like the woman physician who always graduated at the top of her class: in high school, college, and finally in medicine. She never missed church and always did what was expected of her. The word that described her up to that point, she said, was the word *conscientious*. Then a heartrending crisis broke into this ideal life, and for the first time she became a Christian. And the difference was that the word she used to describe herself then was *yielding*.

Her life introduces the meaning of *grace*. No matter how good we are, or how hard we try, we are all dormant without a change of heart, which only grace can accomplish. We are absolutely as incapable of lifting a finger to save ourselves as Simon Peter. We require as much assistance as a baby does at birth, which is why Christ insisted that proper Nicodemus needed another birth. Not a teacher, nor an example, not even a friend, can provide us enough help; the very finest of us, perhaps they more than anyone else, need a Saviour. As Paul explains: "For by grace are ye saved through faith; and that not of yourselves: It is the gift of God: Not of works, lest any man should boast" (Ephesians 2:8,9 KJV).

This is not to exalt an inferiority complex, which is an illness requiring treatment. Each healthy child must go through adolescence, which normally requires an exaggerated appreciation of his or her own gifts of beauty, intelligence, height, or muscle. And if someone suffers the loss of this crucial stage of self-confidence, others later must therapeutically supply this ego deficiency. But sooner or later each person must come to recognize, along with the conscientious woman physician, that her help is in the name of the Lord, and her need for that is as high as "the heavens are above the earth."

Grace is defined as "unmerited favor," and one of the most amazing things about grace, perhaps the most definitive, is the way it touches lives we've casually dismissed as irreligious, even sacrilegious—or people who express faith so differently we cannot find it under a proper heading in our book. For instance I have been accustomed to interpreting Mark Twain as an irascible old cynic whose bitterness against everybody, including God, swept all love away until he scratched down *Letters to Earth* and died. This is the position to which most graduate schools of English ascribe, and which I fully endorsed. Not anymore.

Only God knows what is in someone's heart, and my son has corrected my reading of the aged Twain by stressing the importance of his neglected autobiography. There is rich praise of God implied in it, which I deal with at more length in my book *Before You Call, I Will Answer*. Twain even uses the word *blessed*. His *Autobiography* was written, as he said, "literally from the grave," and it is not good ammunition for anyone setting out to prove Twain's profanity.

Twain's account of how he secured permission for his beloved Livy Langdon's hand from her formidable father is one of the most striking parables of grace that I have encountered in life or literature.

> In a private talk Mr. Langdon called my attention to something I had already noticed—which was that I was an almost entirely unknown person; that no one around about knew me except Charley, and he was too young to be a reliable judge of men; that I was from the other side of the continent and that only those people out there would be able to furnish me a character, in case I had one—so he asked me for references. I furnished them, and he said we would now suspend our industries and could go away and wait until he could write to those people and get answers.
>
> In due course answers came. I was sent

for and we had another private conference. I had referred him to six prominent men, among them two clergymen (these were all San Franciscans), and he himself had written to a bank cashier who had in earlier years been a Sunday-school superintendent in Elmira and well known to Mr. Langdon. The results were not promising. All those men were frank to a fault. They not only spoke in disapproval of me but they were quite unnecessarily and exaggeratedly enthusiastic about it. One clergyman (Stebbins) and that ex-Sunday-school superintendent (I wish I could recall his name) added to their black testimony the conviction that I would fill a drunkard's grave. It was just one of those usual long-distance prophecies. There being no time limit, there is no telling how long you may have to wait. I have waited until now and the fulfillment seems as far away as ever.

The reading of the letters being finished, there was a good deal of a pause and it consisted largely of sadness and solemnity. I couldn't think of anything to say. Mr. Langdon was apparently in the same condition. Finally he raised his handsome head, fixed his clear and candid eye upon me and said: "What kind of people are these? Haven't you a friend in the world?" I said, "Apparently not." Then he said: "I'll be your friend my-self. Take the girl. I know you better than they do."

Grace is not impersonal. By grace we mean Christ. The hymn we celebrate sings not simply of a free handout; it was from "Him." Mary Magdalene's seven devils were not removed by mail. Sanity returned to that raving maniac, Legion, not by a message, but by a visit. I don't believe Jesus would have broken Nicodemus away from the opposition without a heart-to-heart talk. The centurion had Rome behind him, but to save his slave, he needed not simply an answer, but Someone to say the word. At different times in our lives we're all as desperate as the thief. What would he have done without Someone hanging beside him? Grace isn't automatic. It isn't oozing from the pores of the universe; it pours out upon us, often through others, from the blood and the love of Christ.

Forgive me for mentioning my personal experiences, but they are the only kind I have ever had; and really all I have to offer in this book is my own experience in the light of the Scripture through Christ.

My father rescued me from the streets by moving my sister and mother and me to a farm far back in the Ohio hills. My sister and I walked a farm lane over a mile long to get the school bus, and of course, we enjoyed the society of friends and teachers there. But those long winter evenings and the interminable summers were spent, really, in almost complete isolation, except for the horses that pulled the plow, cultivator or mower, and my dog that was closer to me, day or night, than any other creature I've ever known. I was alone in the world, which made it easier for me to see that it was enchanted by the presence of God.

When I analyze any strength or faith I have now, my mind goes back to the splendor of those adolescent summers when happily I was forced to make it alone. Others tell me they found Him in the Scriptures. I found alone the One the Scriptures later explained to me. Intellectually, I still had a long pilgrimage, but my heart, I was to realize later, had found its resting place. It was not until after the road to Emmaus, that the two believers exclaimed: ". . . Did not our heart burn within us . . ." (Luke 24:32 KJV).

At sea in World War II, we took turns standing watch as officer of the deck of our LST 122. At twenty I was certainly no seasoned seaman, even though at night I was alone and completely in charge of that old washtub. We were flagship in a convoy with two other LSTs, which were following us from Shanghai to Subic Bay in the Philippines.

We had been having difficulty with our diesel engines. They would stop without warning, leaving us vulnerable to collision from behind, although by day the officers on watch could see clearly enough to steer out of each other's way. What if our engines went out at night? Then before we knew it, the ship behind could plow into us in the confusion. Ships of such tonnage are not easily stopped and could easily cause a maritime disaster.

One afternoon, a young fellow officer, like an angel from heaven, forced me to think through the best procedure to deal with that contingency. We decided if that should happen on either of our watches that night, we would instruct the helmsman to make a "right standard rudder," phoning the ships behind to continue on course.

Sure enough, that night on my watch, about 2 A.M., the throbbing of the engines stopped vibrating the deck, and it was obvious we were rapidly losing way, with the next ship gaining on us. The young quartermaster flew down from the flight bridge, beside himself with fear; immediately I put into effect exactly what I believe God had told me to do; and everything worked out precisely as planned. I shamefully kept God's help to myself and pocketed all the credit for remaining heroically cool and collected, while seeming to have averted a disaster at sea.

Such an experience makes me realize that there must be many more gracious deliverances hidden by my own arrogance and vanity, but God has also been quite graphic at times in calling such assists to my attention.

I moved to St. Augustine to be minister of Flagler Presbyterian Church, with the understanding that my family would not be required to live in the goldfish bowl manse that was next door. The manse was pointed out by the carriage and tourist trains, and was, as well, a woman killer with three floors that our physician did not feel was a judicious responsibility for my wife and mother of four.

However, upon arrival, I discovered that the trustees of the church were not enthusiastic about our abandoning the old manse in which they had so much invested, where their ministers had always lived as long as they could remember. In fact, one trustee, who also happened at the same time to be an elder on the session, was absolutely adamant in his opposition to such a radical change in their long-standing church policy. He was obviously the determined ringleader of the opposition. As long as he was around, we would be in that manse no matter what the effect on the pulpit committee's promise to me, or on my wife's health.

What do you do when you are up against something that may not be a matter of life and death, but still involves one's courage and the health of the family? While I have often failed due to lack of faith and by plain mismanagement, I decided not to panic, nor overreact this time but to mention it to God. I was prompted to invite this recalcitrant opponent out to lunch alone.

Lunch began formally, as my antagonist and I circled each other waiting for an opportunity to open fire. He and I were about the same age and someone had told me that he had also been in the Pacific in World War II. Armed with that, I asked about his service. He had been a flyer for the navy. When I told him I too was navy, there was a noticeable lessening of tension. Before we knew it, we discovered we had both been aboard the old *Saratoga,* an aircraft carrier, during the worst typhoon ever to hit the Pacific. It had sent many ships to the bottom, and we both recalled that the Saratoga had rolled to her critical list of twenty-seven degrees and, after what seemed an eternity, finally righted herself.

There is among shipmates the closest kinship, particularly when they have gone through a crisis at sea together. I do not quite know how to describe this family tie that occurs among sailors. This navy pilot, for all his previous opposition, was one of those who would have died before letting a shipmate down, particularly one who had shared this near-fateful voyage. We must have remained at that lunch table 'til the middle of the afternoon. And when we parted, he wept and his arms were around me.

At our next board meeting when the matter of the housing came up, my old shipmate stated, as positively as he had before, negatively, "We're going to have to do whatever Dave wants." And that settled it. There was no further problem. And many another potential problem melted away from the blessing of that friendship born "aboard" the old *Saratoga.* I could not possibly dismiss all the assistance that came from that as mere coincidence. It was a big piece of the amazing grace I received, as though Someone were looking after one who was not competent to look after himself.

However, the most amazing grace given me with the exception of Christ and my family, was my commission to become a writer. It is to me what the burning bush was to Moses, and almost as impossible for me to grasp still, as it was that morning for Gideon when the fleece he left outside was dry while the grass was soaked with dew.

I realize now that I had wanted to be a writer ever since I was a child. I am sure my dearest mother spoiled me into thinking I was something special. However, while I finally taught courses in English literature for several years both in high school and in college, several things conspired to bring my studies at the graduate school of English to a crashing halt. And it was with a broken heart and my tail between my legs that I left for divinity school, as though I had no place else left to go.

God's forcing me to become a preacher seemed, as I believe it did to Jeremiah, the worst fate that could happen to one on earth. And while, as I will mention, the inspiration of Albert Schweitzer had begun its work on me to guide me into divinity school, I was coming to my new calling because God pressured me to do it. Writing, my first love, had been torn from me. And while I had every intention of serving God the best I could in this alien world of ministry, I entered it as though without my arms.

However, I was no sooner through seminary and

into my first pastorate than I was finding out what had never occurred to me before, that a minister is writing for every Sunday service. And I was also discovering that despite my change of vocation, I still had arms; and my writing hopes, hope against hope, were returning to me.

My first major effort was a sermon on the Lord's Prayer. Somehow I felt that it had merit beyond my little church's pulpit, and while secular periodicals are not usually begging to peek into minister's sermon barrels, I permitted my wife to submit my sermon to several periodicals, where, as any fool would have known, it was hastily returned, as though it were forbidden material. The returned manuscript apparently did not deserve the dignity of a personal message. Clipped to it in each case was only a mass-produced pink slip, which reported that the piece had been received and found "unsuitable for our editorial needs."

Not seeming very intelligent I sent the same piece to *Reader's Digest*. They returned it with a pink slip. Then I sent it to *Life* magazine, which was then a weekly, and they too, of course, returned it, although I believe it was with a blue slip.

For some reason I cannot fathom to this day, for it still seems so brainless and absurd, I decided to mail it back again to *Life* to another editor listed a little higher on the masthead. I mailed a cover letter with the manuscript suggesting they use it as an editorial.

Life answered me this time with graciousness that

scorched a little. In part their letter read: "Our editorials are written by our own staff." However, I guess only death itself stops the kind of pathological fixation that seemed to possess me. I mailed the "Lord's Prayer" to an even more senior editor of *Life*.

Several weeks after that I was studying in the library of the University of Cincinnati, with the literary fiasco of my Lord's Prayer sermon completely buried. It was a very proper library, littered everywhere with signs marked, SILENCE. No one was ever paged in that place, and besides I was an unknown young preacher, a complete stranger to them—a rejected refugee from the literary world who had sought sanctuary in a corner there to read a real author.

Suddenly, I heard my name being paged: "Mr. Redding, you have a phone call at the front desk." I responded numbly, stood there as in a dream while the voice on the other end said: "This is John Jessup, chief editorial writer for *Life* magazine. We like your 'Lord's Prayer' and want to use it as our editorial for our Easter issue. Would an honorarium of seven hundred and fifty dollars be acceptable?" I replied, "I think it would."

All of my writing came from that publication of my sermon on the Lord's Prayer. *Reader's Digest* reprinted it the following year as their Easter feature. It was translated and reprinted abroad. The opportunity to write other articles, for other periodicals, as well as again for *Life*, came because of the credentials established by my sermon on the Lord's Prayer. Seeing the article in *Life*, the editors of Revell wrote to me about writing my first book. They were to publish my first five books, and the latest two.

All of my writing has come, my entire career in writing, from that remarkable opening Christ Himself generously made for me with His own prayer. Can you imagine how I feel about the Lord Jesus every time I repeat His prayer, when my lifetime longing for writing comes from there? He let me ride into my city on Him. "Trespasses," "Debts," "Our Father," "The power and the glory." These words are precious to me, primarily because He said them to save us all, but also because they are the very words by which He employed me in the profession I love and never would have had, had His heart not gone out to me that day in the library. "Amazing Grace, how sweet the sound that saved a wretch like me."

5.

A Rose Will
Grow Anywhere

Annie Pinney remembered a true-life story that happened to her mother, Suzanna, following the First World War, when she was a little girl of five in France. Suzanna's mother led her by the hand through the shelled ruins of their village. Out of the midst of some rubble a gorgeous rose was blooming. Then the war-torn mother told the little child something she would never forget: "Remember, Suzanna, a rose will grow anywhere."

Earthlings need to hear repeatedly this phenomenal news. We've always belonged to an endangered species, no sooner emerging from epidemics of marauding Vikings and wanton typhoid than we're doomed by self-induced stress or nuclear burnout. Before life there looms, we fear, an empty void, and after death, a trackless desert: "Remember, Suzanna, a rose will grow anywhere." Could there be a better introduction to our belief in the One to whom Scripture refers as the Rose of Sharon, who came to this desolate planet and left His lingering fragrance as a reminder and a proof of His return?

Recently I made a speaking tour of Episcopal churches in Texas, intending, I suppose, to enlighten "the wild, wild west" with the finer points of faith. As you can imagine, I was taught a lesson or two that far outweighed the homiletic freight I carried. The text of the sermon Texas preached to me was along the lines of Paul's words: ". . . all things work together for good to those who love God . . ." (Romans 8:28). "All things?" Some things. Perhaps a few things. No. "All things."

My night in Austin was memorable. I stayed in the guest apartment of a remarkable couple whose hospitality touched my heart. He was from a family of Texas engineers. She had been a nurse and still spoke with a lovely Swiss accent. I was to have breakfast with them the next morning in their suite on the next floor. There was a Swiss chocolate bar on the pillow, and on the lamp stand beside the bed there was a new book, *The Words of Albert Schweitzer*, introduced by Norman Cousins.

Somehow the thoughtful combination of the Swiss

chocolate and the Swiss-German missionary doctor affected me deeply. Schweitzer was the one who had literally lifted me out of my pagan preoccupation with the field of English and landed me in divinity school. My aunt had mailed me his book, *Out of My Life and Thought,* and it oriented me to the Christian faith. My father had been a circuit-riding minister who had lost his faith partly because of the pettiness of the church, and partly because of the problems of higher criticism, which had undercut his belief in the Bible as the Word of God. Schweitzer's book returned the Christian faith to my disillusioned father as it introduced it to me.

A rose could grow in my lost father and agnostic me, but think of Schweitzer. He had been a learned theologian around the turn of the century who had set out to prove that Jesus suffered from pathological delusions. Instead, his research developed into *The Quest for the Historical Jesus,* which brought credibility to the serious study of Christ in the twentieth century.

Schweitzer got so carried away with his subject that he decided to serve Christ "without having to talk" in the darkest hole he could find in Africa. He abandoned his doctorates in several fields where he had already distinguished himself, acquired a degree in medicine, and poured out his long life in a hospital he built and maintained for almost half a century in Lambaréne in Africa. Cousins' new edition, in my hands that night, included the *Grand Docteur's* moving decision: "I decided to use my life as my argument." "Always remember, Suzanna, a rose will grow anywhere."

The next morning at breakfast my lesson continued. My hostess turned out to have been Schweitzer's surgical nurse for his last three years in Africa. While I absorbed that, we discussed the momentous impact Schweitzer made on the Western world. I recalled that when I had arrived in seminary, it had seemed to me that all my new colleagues there had enrolled because of Schweitzer too. "Had there really been anyone else," I suggested, "whose life and thought had fought harder against the blanket of despair flung over the school of English by existentialists such as Jean Paul Sartre, and from under which I had crawled to enter divinity school?"

Then my hostess asked, "Did you know that Jean Paul Sartre and Albert Schweitzer were first cousins?" "No." "Yes, they used to have the most terrible arguments." Then she said something that went straight to the roots of my being. "Did you know that Sartre became a Christian before he died?" "No. I don't know anything." "Yes!"

Had Schweitzer, who set out to prove the Lord's insanity, in the end been the one to defrock the "Pope of despair," and make him Christ's? All I know is what the mother said to her little girl: "Remember, Suzanna, a rose will grow anywhere."

At Liberty Church prospective members meet in a circle, not to be lectured but to make friends. And this neglected priority is accomplished by sharing finally, some jagged piece of their lives, perhaps still sticking in their craw. Jesse Laird of Montana taught me that the act of love, the love commanded by Christ, is when someone coughs up a lump in his throat, not for others to discuss or critique, but for them to understand in silence. There can be no pushing, nor curiosity, but if someone volunteers, "I'm illegitimate, and it's been a cross for me to carry," then it triggers painful confidences from each one as he takes his turn around the circle. So, someone will say, "My daughter had an illegitimate child," and someone else may add, "I'm not illegitimate, but the odd ball in our family."

Everyone in such a group must be free to "pass," and the mood must be delicately established by the proper sequence of these questions: 1. "How did you get your middle name?" 2. "What do you remember as the place of warmth when you were a child?" The third question, after the two ice breakers, almost invariably plunges everyone deep into each other's heart; 3. "When did you first run into God?"

Mysteriously one finds that almost everyone ran into God when in trouble. Each person, while completely free to say, "I pass," finds his turn almost irresistible, and often, filled with tears. Some are weeping already as their turn approaches: "At fourteen I came down with polio"; an excessively overweight man reduces the rest of us as he sighs, "Please believe I tried." A lovely woman executive gets it out haltingly: "My folks told me that God was like math. If I am to make it now, I have got to find a God who is more than math." So often the rose grows best in what seems to us the dung that life has heaped upon us. Our suffering is not proof of God's absence as the college sophomore insists. Few ever came to God any other way.

Of all the magnificent stars and planets from which God had to choose, He selected tiny Earth to visit, and of all the places in the time of the Roman Empire, He picked neither palace, nor campus, nor Olympus, but a barren, broken, bickering little leftover piece of land, called Herod's spittoon. The Dead Sea is the lowest spot on the face of the earth, geographically. Its surface is 1,300 feet below sea level. It was near this unappealing geographical and political situation that the stable was located in which Mary delivered the Saviour of the world. Who would have thought that a rose would ever grow there?

I suppose a certain kind of Horatio Alger story could have utilized that rude beginning to advantage, but in the Old, Old Story the prosperity and the riches never came to that poor boy. After the stable He had to face the sarcasm of the educated Pharisees, then the condescension of Pilate, and finally the scorn and spit of a riotous mob.

The ugliest and most despicable death that those masters of torture, the Romans, could contrive was the crucifixion. No nightmare, neither Auschwitz, nor Andersonville, nor Hiroshima absolutely pierces the heart of man as does the infamy, the degradation, and the horror of the Cross. And that is where the One we call the Rose of Sharon was nailed.

What seems to us proof that there is no God—headlines about half the world starving, hell opening up in the center of our great cities, and in the spiraling cocaine traffic—all excavates more room for God. Somehow despair destines people to God. As we have already appreciated, opposition makes more Christians behind the Iron Curtain than we successfully bribe in the West.

But roses require planting. A contemporary Christian entertainer and musical evangelist has confessed that he was once a priest of Satan in a church of 2,000 members, filled with hatred against God. By a series of cataclysmic events in his life, including a blackout caused by a binge of drugs, he returned to consciousness to find himself in the navy and, of all things, bunking with two rather insistent Christian believers.

He warned them against their impatient evangelism, but though they spoke with good-hearted humor, they wouldn't stop. One day he fought back by knocking one of them down; and as the Christian fell he bloodied his head badly on the sharp corner of a hard bench, and it knocked him out. His buddies immediately hauled him off to the hospital, leaving the shaken priest of Satan sitting there staring at his missionaries' open Bible that had been providentially left behind.

He took a closer look at the page to which the Bible was open. The verse that looked up at him was, "For God so loved the world, that he gave his only begotten Son, that whosoever believeth in him should not perish, but have everlasting life" (John 3:16 KJV). One word in that passage went straight to his heart and knocked him out of Satan's corner and into Christ's. It was that loving word, *whosoever*. He identified with that word. He was a "whosoever." Despite some regrettable impertinence, those two bunkmates had succeeded in planting a rose in a hostile garden.

Wouldn't Mother Teresa have done more good in a neat convent in Europe where she would have had room to get her feet under a nice table and into a neat bed at night? No. Roses seem to do better in predicaments where they're not wanted, where there is no hope.

The sight of this five foot nun ministering to the dying moved city officials to give her a dharmsala (inn) opposite Calcutta's famous temple of Kali, the Hindu goddess of death. But many Brahmins objected to having a Christian center so near a Hindu holy place and some stoned the windows, demanding her removal. One morning, Mother Teresa picked up a man dying of cholera outside the temple and looked after him until his death. The man was a temple priest, and her compassion so moved another Hindu holy man that he knelt before her and said: "For thirty years I have served the goddess Kali in her temple. Now the goddess stands before me."

Newsweek (October 29, 1979)

A few pages back I mentioned the full-sized cross-beam the old curator in St. Augustine spiked into place each Maundy Thursday evening, then hung on it a crown of thorns. On Easter morning the old man limped slowly down the aisle and took down the crown of thorns, replacing it with a red rose. I asked a friend in St. Augustine one time when she had become a Christian. She replied that it had been the moment one Easter when the old man pinned the rose to the cross.

The rose and the Cross. What a combination! Somehow nothing less will grow the rose. Remember Thomas was incapable of belief until the One who'd been crucified forced the hand of Thomas onto His nail prints, and into His side. Not until then did Thomas cry, "My Lord, and my God."

"Lo, how a rose ere blooming, from tender stem hath sprung."

6

Three Unsuspected
Traitors

Napoleon may not have died from natural causes in exile on St. Helena but, as more recent research suggests, from arsenic poisoning by a jealous member of his staff. The arsenic was successfully poured into Napoleon's personal wine cask. The dosage was lethal but so gradual as to be all but undetectable.

The Communists are not the chief threat to Christianity. "We have met the enemy and he is us." Many people singing "Amazing Grace" don't mean it, they laugh at its belief in the miraculous, at the naive idea that a personal God is doing anything specific to change our lives. Typical church members would never think of taking "amazing grace" literally. They condemn such a concept of God as anthropomorphic; anyone who so believes is considered by such critics to be an anachronism. Solzhenitsyn is thus dismissed as a nineteenth-century man. Such condescension has a lethal effect on our faith.

However, I value scholarship in proper perspective. I hold the position here of C. S. Lewis, that blessed apostle to skeptics who has helped rescue so many of us from both the mania of liberalism, and the paranoia of rigid conservatism. Lewis, for instance, appreciates the contributions of linguists and archaeologists who have done much to enlighten our study of the Bible. The faithful historian is of great assistance in giving us the context in which Scripture was written, in describing the people in biblical times, and in clarifying other social and political forces that operated on their lives.

Our quarrel with the scholars is not with their scholarship, but with the categorical disbelief of some of them in the wonders reported in the Bible. This book wants to encourage the widest possible interpretation of what it means to be a Christian. Charity calls for the utmost tolerance; humility recognizes the severe limitations on our own point of view; love sees so much good in others. But we must never lose faith in the power and the glory of God glimpsed now in the wondrous details of our daily lives.

While we must forgive where we differ, we cannot agree. And we cannot give an inch on our belief in grace, and in our amazement. Christ Himself is an incredible miracle. And our faith is deeply involved in His impossible resurrection from the dead, in the astounding instances of the miraculous presented in the New Testament, and continuing to happen around us now, both promising and preparing us for that most stupendous of all wonders yet to be realized in His return.

So we detest, far more than any other danger, anything that erodes our belief in His amazing grace. And in this chapter we want to unmask and destroy three innocent-looking monsters that are getting away with murder.

Beware of *pettiness.* We say petty cash, meaning small. Stealing petty cash is petty larceny. Napoleon only took petty arsenic. And we are all tempted to engage in petty Christianity. Instead of keeping our eyes on Jesus, and what great things He has done, we become preoccupied by trifles, such as fussing over the color of the church carpet, getting distracted or bogged down in the miscellaneous. "Woe unto you, scribes and Pharisees, hypocrites! for ye pay tithe of mint and anise and cummin, and have omitted the weightier matters of the law ..." (Matthew 23:23 KJV).

We try to console ourselves, because we're not a murderer like Moses, an adulterer like David, or even money mad like Zaccheus, but we can be worse off toying with Christ. Instead of dying for Him, or selling all we have, or turning everything over to Him, we'll sleep through an hour a week for Him, or discuss the dating of the Gospel of Mark by the hour for Him. Or we'll keep busy feathering our own spiritual nest, while abandoning the rest. Mother Teresa stays up all night for some poor nobody. I content myself with bringing a covered dish.

Our sins are none the less potent for being petty. We break the commandment not to kill with such shrewdness we fool ourselves into innocence by tiny cuts instead of mortal blows. We actually think we're all right on this since we don't use a tomahawk anymore. But almost all of us are small-time killers in a far more obnoxious way than excused the righteous fury of Moses. At least *I* am guilty of these petty little put-downs day after day. The sneaky way we do it is by nibbling at each other's ears, 'til they're trimmed. As though we were, as Albert Camus suggested, like piranha, a tropical fish, that devours its victims in tiny little bites, like millions of mosquitoes. The jaws we need to fear are not the sharks, but belong to the tiny "no-see-ums" as they are called in Florida, none the less malarial for their size.

"Did you ever kill anyone?" "Oh, no, we're good people, not a gun in the house." All the tiny little fish with the tiny little teeth. God Almighty have mercy, for our backbiting, or our sarcasm, if we can whoop up enough consensus, we'll get rid of folks far more ingeniously as though we were a spiritual Mafia. Like Napoleon's arsenic, it is all very subtle and difficult to trace.

Think of someone, such as your own wife, or sister, whom you've depreciated. You're not guilty of battering or abusing them, or are you? "All I said was, 'That's very interesting,' " and yet I know it cut and is still quivering in them like a dagger, and must be withdrawn. "He's such a good husband," and yet day after day he whittles away at that dear wife who used to be so pretty. He's no caveman with a club, he's killing her with toothpicks. She died from scratches etched on her heart. He's so clever with his biting comments, along with the way he raises his eyebrows. He's killing her with those eyebrows.

So that you may suspect how petty I am in one respect, I read P. G. Wodehouse. He's not Paul Tillich or William Shakespeare. Wodehouse roasts his sub-hero, Bertie Wooster, who "knows he's a silly [fool] but hopes you won't mind." Bertie is an oaf financed by a legacy. His life is consumed by the most inane banalities: how to get Gussie tanked up enough to drown his shyness at addressing the private girls' school commencement. If it weren't so sad it would be funny, and if it weren't so funny we'd never be able to endure how sad it is.

If Bertie won't wear the combo slacks and spats Jeeves, his butler, puts out, Jeeves pouts, and so Bertie petulantly wears them. I used to think Wodehouse was writing about the spare-tire scion of the British aristocracy, but staring at my schedule now, and remembering what I said at dinner, and my ineffectiveness with the family that used to live next door, I'm afraid to ask, "Is it I?"

Those who know their Bible will be bombarded by instances. There's the elder brother ranting and raving over the prodigal's getting supper. He could care less that his brother is back alive. The elder brother appears without hope, love, or joy. He keeps busy ticking off what he assumes all the money went for.

Then there's the man in Jesus' parable who owes a huge debt. The creditor could have jailed the debtor and his family for it. Instead the creditor magnanimously forgives it all and lets the debtor go. But the debtor turns right around and jails someone who owed him petty cash. This story was Christ's condemnation of pettiness, as well as refusal to forgive. (*See* Matthew 18:21–35.)

Jesus ridiculed the Pharisees for their pettiness: "Who strain out a gnat and swallow a camel" (Matthew 23:24). I waste my time trying to figure out who hit me with that tomato. I keep forgetting that something bigger is going on than record sales, or attendance, or my sore toe.

Can you believe how magnanimous Christ was? He even offered communion to Judas, and washed his feet along with the rest. It was not in Christ to catalogue others' mistakes. He did not have time to detail lists against people: "Father, forgive them" were His last words.

The second traitor I identify is *pedantry*. He usually gets away scot-free while we attack a careful selection of agreed upon sins in which we cannot be incriminated. A pedagogue is a teacher, but a pedant is "someone who reads to be thought learned." Isak Dinesen, the extraordinary Danish novelist, wrote *Out of Africa* from firsthand experience on a coffee plantation there. With rare insight she sensed that the black man rightly feared the white man because of the white man's pedantry.

To the untouched black man in Africa the wind is like a sister. The white man makes a weather report out of it. The black man loved the wind on his face, the white man puts it in an encyclopedia. The black man lives with the wind, and thrives on it, while the white man catalogues it. While the black man is melting into the sunrise, the pedantic white man is keeping records and doing paperwork by artificial light.

The pedantry of the Pharisees wearied Christ, who, He said, "For a pretense make long prayers." He called them on their masquerades: "You adorn the monuments of the righteous" . . . "fill up then the measure of your father's guilt." "You cleanse the outside of the cup, . . . but inside . . . full of extortion and self-indulgence." (*See* Matthew 23.)

Prayer meetings suffer and die from pedantry. Peter's prayers raised the dead in Acts; pretended prayers put people to sleep. Churches refer to inactive members as deadwood. People can fill pews and put a

little something in the offering and still be deadwood.
Deadwood means saying the right words fruitlessly.
That is the way a minister dies, saying all the right
words, going through all the right motions—but his
heart has stopped beating for anybody. Spurgeon
spoke of a minister "who was so dry that he would
make a good martyr, for he would burn well."

One time a young mother came to see me about the
baptism of her child. She requested that I baptize her
child without using any religious language. There was
a time when I would have been deeply offended by
such a request, for the Lord's sake. But I knew why
this young mother had made this seemingly sacrilegious plea.

Her parents were the most pedantic people imagin-
able. They never missed church, never failed to do the
right thing, but their hearts were cold as stone. To this
young mother all their religious language was torture,
for it wasn't true to their lives; beautiful memory
verses were a facade drawn over empty souls. "The
letter kills, but the Spirit gives life," as Paul said in 2
Corinthians 3:6.

Wasn't it pedantry for which Christ accused the
Pharisees? "You travel sea and land to win one proselyte, and when he is won, you make him twice as
much a son of hell as yourselves" (Matthew 23:15).
Pedantry diverts the faith into a lifeless realm devoid of
art. There is no beauty in it. A pedantic man will have
no children spiritually. He is sterile and uninteresting.

One of hell's chief characteristics is boredom. C. S. Lewis believed that there was no worse sin than to make Jesus boring. Such a tragedy means we have killed Him off and come up with a corpse. Pedantry will do everything decently and in order, but it is a killjoy. The church will not collapse from the more scandalous forms of evil; it will die from boredom.

We came to life on earth. It is life that Jesus gives us, but the pedantic approach will preoccupy us by a guilt trip. Pedantry is as subtle as arsenic, making us dwell on the devil of it, what's wrong with us. To the contrary Jesus is the Lord of Life whose chief purpose is to raise the dead.

The third traitor is *presumption*. It is a nasty form of the pride of Lucifer, which slips neatly by the guard of the most careful Christian. The Bible has quite a bit to say about it: "Keep back thy servant from presumptuous sins," prays Psalm Nineteen.

The most famous use of this word was when Stanley, the newspaperman, finally found the long-lost missionary doctor and explorer deep in Africa: "Doctor Livingstone, I presume." I presume he said it, though some say it is not warranted by the facts, which goes to show what presumption is—taking a lot for granted. Presumption takes liberties without invitation or permission, takes advantage of other people's weakness, takes over where we're not authorized, where we have no God-given right.

Presumption goes downhill from here. Eve presumed it was permissible to eat the apple, since the serpent said so. Adam's descendants built a tower to top Heaven, and God toppled them into babbling idiots for such arrogant presumption as to sneak up to Heaven on their own. "You shall not tempt the Lord your God" (Matthew 4:7).

Presumption is one of faith's worst and least-suspected enemies. An evangelist presumes he's saved. And he often presumes you are not, even presuming to know that now is the time for you to be saved. And here *I* am presuming that evangelists are like this. But I do believe that churches, even prayer meetings and Bible studies, are often characterized by presumption. The seemingly religious person presumes to speak for everybody, makes up prayers often nosing into business only God should know. A minister can be filled with presumption and yet get away with it under a heavy coating of the most unctuous manners. The Lord knows we can abuse His Word, and even make our heaviest offering to our own advantage.

A young man told me a true story of one minister's presumption. The youth was sitting in the waiting room of the church office to pick up his mother following a meeting. The senior minister peeked out and presuming the young man was someone else, called him in.

Before his guest could explain, the minister, in a strong voice and with his eye glued to the steeple outside the window, congratulated him on his life-changing decision to go into the ministry. Finally the minister, who waved away every feeble gesture, solemnly requested this fine young man to kneel, so, as he said, "I can pray you into the Gospel ministry."

The presumptuous minister pressed the boy's head down with his strong ordaining hands and prayed "that this young man of God might carry the torch of Christ even to the depths of darkest Africa." As one could have predicted, that young man fled that office and was never seen near that waiting room again.

My uncle went for me when I was fourteen. "David, are you saved?" Of course he presumed he was, and I, of course, presumed he was not, knowing of his cruelty to his son, who was my cousin and boyhood chum. Perhaps, I presumed too easily that he wasn't saved, for most likely my cousin needed discipline, and for all I know the only thing wrong with my uncle was his whip hand, and his belligerent manner.

But "everybody talking about Heaven ain't a goin' there," and neither are all those who quote this old spiritual against them, as I am doing here.

The most lavish praise of God can be suspected of presumption. When the woman cried out to Christ, "Blessed is the womb that bore you, and the breasts that nursed you," Jesus rebuked her, "Yea, blessed are they who hear the Word of God and *do* it." (*See* Luke 11:27, 28.) Going to church and singing God's praises loudly can be sin, if done presumptuously.

Ministers may lambaste those who don't darken the

door of the church. But hear the Word of God: "The prophet who presumes to speak a word in My name, which I have not commanded him to speak . . . that prophet shall die" (Deuteronomy 18:20). Such a warning should be enough to silence some of us some of the time even when we think what we are saying is "for their own good."

Paul Tournier, that grand old Swiss therapist who has taught us all so much, was asked if after he became a Christian he remained proud. He answered that he was still proud, but that now he believed he recognized it and prayed to be forgiven for it. Presumption is like refuse, which we keep producing and must be continually carried off.

My sister and I have always been devoted to each other. I was four years older, so she was my shadow when we were growing up. But that's it: I unconsciously subordinated her to the position of shadow. In recent years she has been able to share with me my presumption in claiming first place, the birthright. I was the firstborn son. When my sister and I were introduced to guests, my name was mentioned first, my grades were asked for first, and my place at the table was to my father's right. I was more talkative, so I presumed to speak for her; I even presumed to make choices for her. I did it agreeably as part of my scarcely noticeable intimidation: "Mary, you prefer to go to this particular movie too, don't you?" Not until recent years was I able to comprehend that I was obviously standing on her foot all those years, thinking myself so noble and understanding a brother. "Lord, cleanse thou me from secret faults" (Psalms 19:12 KJV).

We can write presumptuous obituaries and epitaphs, even attempting, I suppose, to barge into heaven with a hearty: "God the Father Almighty, I presume." Such an attitude is far worse than arsenic for us. This snide little trio of sins—pettiness, pedantry, and presumption—are subtly poisoning souls who presume they're safely keeping His commandments. For those of us who have ears to hear He has suggested a more modest approach, "Don't sit down in the best place" (*see* Luke 14:8), which allows Him the authority of the One who, as our creed declares, "Shall come to judge the quick and the dead."

7

*Eating Your
Heart Out*

Villains such as pettiness, pedantry, and presumption have been eating the heart out of the church. Even our country has lost heart. Not only is heart disease the leading cause of death in our country, more people die from heart and blood vessel disease than all other causes combined.

Dr. James J. Lynch, in his book *The Broken Heart: The Medical Consequences of Loneliness* (Basic Books, 1977) reports that heart disease is ". . . striking more and more at younger subjects. It will result in the greatest epidemic mankind has ever faced unless we are able to reverse the trend. . . ." Heart trouble hits Americans "under 55 double that of Denmark, Sweden, and Norway and six times higher than that of Japan. . . . What is it about life in the United States?"

The famous government-sponsored Framingham Heart Study unearthed several factors that are like red flags warning that we are in jeopardy of heart trouble. These factors include high blood pressure, elevated serum cholesterol, and cigarette smoking.

But while these factors certainly are closely related to coronary problems, Dr. Lynch and others have been searching for more far-reaching social and religious reasons, particularly in light of studies of such towns as Roseto, Pennsylvania. Dr. Stewart Wolf found that although the people of Roseto violated the Framingham "house rules," consuming far above average numbers of calories as well as committing other cardiological "no-no's," the incidence of heart disease in Roseto was about one-third that of the neighboring communities.

Was it because Roseto, with its largely Italian population, about 1,600 in the 1960s, seemed to be in so many respects, one big happy family? Dr. Lynch, and also Victor Fuchs (*Who Shall Live?* Basic Books, 1974) contrast the states of Nevada and Utah. "In 1960 . . . for white males and females between the ages of 25 and 64, Nevada had by far the highest death rates in the country . . . neighboring Utah . . . has one of the lowest death rates in the country. . . ." How do we account for that?

Dr. Fuchs points out that Utah's predominant group, the Mormons, don't move, don't smoke, don't divorce, don't drink, not even coffee or tea. Nevada, on the other hand, has been one of the divorce and gambling capitals of the United States; a high proportion of the adult population is single; and Nevada has few natives. Only one out of ten residents was born there.

Is the entire United States headed for Las Vegas? What will be the ultimate effect of the single-parent families, the "latchkey" children, the children born out of wedlock?

The above observations are not to condemn any of us; we are just pointing out that the threat of heart disease is not going to be taken care of by jogging, dieting, transplants, and bypasses; our *heartbreak* and *heartache* have something to do with our *sweet heart,* or people being dis*heartened.* These words did not creep into the language for nothing.

Something more than cholesterol is eating our hearts out. What is behind the high blood pressure? Is it loneliness? Estrangement from those who should be dear to us? What causes even so-called religious people to come down with "hurry sickness"? Why do we become frantic achievers who have to do more and more in less and less time, drifting further and further apart from family and friends? And this is as true of up-tight homes as well as broken ones.

It is well-known that the increased mortality among the bereaved is especially high during the first six months after the loss of a loved one.

A growing number of heart specialists seem to be tracing the heart trouble in our time to the tragic disappearance of friendship. Just as infants who have

suddenly lost their mothers waste away with maras-
mus and will not eat, or live even if force-fed, so adults
without hugs or touching, or being warmed by dear
friends, are in coronary danger for their lives.

In *The Broken Heart* we read about a fifty-year-old
man, who was in a deep coma, was near death and
completely paralyzed by a drug known as D-Tubo-
curaine. He was able to breathe only by mechanical re-
spiratory assistance. The doctors reported: "We
watched this man's heart change abruptly when the
nurse held his hand."

The famed coach Bear Bryant was asked to explain
why his teams were winners, with the longest run of
victories in college football history. He said simply, "I
gave them one heartbeat." "Two hearts beat as one"
not only in romantic love, but in buddies in combat in
World War II, and in client and psychiatrist, as shown
by monitors when their minds are not wandering but
enjoying deep rapport. Not even experimentally, can
monkeys make it for long with dolls. We all need someone, as the young Ebenezer Scrooge expressed in the
haunting words from the musical version of *A
Christmas Carol:* "Where is a voice to answer mine
back, where are two shoes that click to my clack?" So
Plato wisely did not confine himself to monologues.
His enduring legacy was the *Dialogues.*

We mentioned the deep intimacy of buddies in
combat. The heroism in war, not only more recently in
Vietnam and in the World Wars, was born not simply

from patriotism when "uncommon valor was a common virtue"; it was because soldiers were fighting for each other's lives. Their courage and sacrifice came from their friendships. What kept them from losing heart was actually love.

We must not allow loneliness to take our country away from us now. Our country is not Washington, D.C.; it is we friends of liberty. It is a spirit that has come from companionship.

I used to think that our country was born out of George Washington's courage and integrity, qualities he certainly enjoyed. But we call him the Father of Our Country, and he could never have been named our father without a bond of affection. Stuart's portrait shows him formidable and forbidding. Our texts stress his strength, but he had to have something more to glue such recalcitrant Yankees and the bickering colonies together.

Recently I waded through Douglas Freeman's *Life of Washington;* it is an eight-volume shelf of books, and I finally found what I was looking for. Washington did have a heart, and that is what stuck our tiny nation together against the chaos of loneliness and despair that nearly swept us under.

Looking back on how we ever got through those hard times, like Valley Forge, George Mason said: "It seemed as though we had been treading on enchanted ground." See if you don't agree that the truly amazing story of the Stars and Stripes growing out of Plymouth

Rock had to do with the enchantment of our hearts for each other and for a friend whom God appointed Father. The place is Yorktown. England had surrendered, and the Revolution was won. The scene I want to share from Douglas Freeman's fifth volume is Washington's farewell to his officers. Here follows the memorable passage that heartened me:

> Twelve o'clock would be a suitable hour and Fraunces' Tavern the most convenient place for saying farewell to the officers . . . Washington wrote no address. . . . Besides, he could not trust himself to read. . . . Already as the hour approached, he was choking with an emotion that even his powerful will could not suppress. When he entered the long room at Fraunces', soon after the clock struck the hour, he found there nearly all the officers who had entered the city on the 25th and all the others who could assemble on short notice. . . . they were typical of the hundreds who had remained at their posts in poverty and shabbiness while their families at home had pinched and patched though speculating neighbors had grown fat. . . .
>
> When the decanters had gone the rounds, Washington, half-choked, said simply: "With a heart full of love and gratitude, I now take

leave of you. I most devoutly wish that your later days may be as prosperous and happy as your former ones have been glorious and honorable."

Then they drank their wine, not aware that in a manner wholly unintended, it was communion.

By the time they had drunk all of it, Washington's emotions had risen so high again that tears were blinding him. "I cannot come to each of you," he said in a faltering voice, "but shall feel obliged if each of you will come and take me by the hand." Chance fixed it that in the absence of Nathaniel Greene, the soldier best entitled to be first among them was nearest at hand—Henry Knox, the man who had brought the cannon over the ice from Ticonderoga, youthful father of the artillery corps, the one senior officer of whom it could be said that in eight years of service he had not given his General an hour of needless concern.

Knox stepped forward silently and held out his hand; Washington extended his own but as he looked into those honest eyes and remembered what Knox had meant to him, he could not say farewell with a handshake. Impulsively he put his arms around Knox and, weeping, kissed his chief of artillery.

Once done, this had, of course, to be done with all, from Steuben to the youngest officer. With streaming eyes they came up to him, received the same embrace and passed on ... Not a man had the bad taste to attempt any expression of thanks or of admiration. . . .

When the last weeping officer had received his embrace, the General walked across the room, raised his arm in an all-inclusive, silent farewell and passed through the door, out of the tavern, between the open ranks of a guard of honor, then along the streets to Whitehall.

The church can no longer get away with pedantic ritual and spiritual trivia. Bible experts are drying up and dying from loneliness or lack of true companionship which can only be won in a common purpose such as we just read. Record-breaking church attendance is sick if we are simply isolated spectators, as alienated from those beside us as strangers waiting in a bus station.

In recent years we have mistreated the church as a second-rate learning center rather than a family around a supper table, or "like a mighty army." Phrases like Bible study and church school introduce church as a hobby, not as our living room. A hierarchy has sprung up in the church based on biblical knowledge and expertise in church law. And while some teaching is certainly necessary, its overemphasis has diverted us far from home and battlefield, which is where the church should be.

In the 1960s Keith Miller had a heart-to-heart talk with God and exploded into new life. It had more to do with his getting beside God and next to others than a breakthrough in knowledge. He called this event *The Taste of New Wine,* and it was the beginning of a movement back to God Himself, and not another book about God.

And the way to draw near to God is to draw near to each other. Church membership classes should be turned into an adventure in friendship. Wanting to know about church must become second to getting next to each other and to God. Our minister is not to be a fact finder who showers us with his ecclesiasticism from the pulpit; we must know how to "break bread together on our knees." The minister must permit the familiar rite of crumbs and juice to become a mighty banquet of the Spirit that makes hearts pound back together. How can we call it communion when we can't even communicate? Communion is when you trust someone with some of your agony, when you share some Valley Forge together. Communion is when hearts beat as one under the same Lord, bearing the same load blessed already by the beyond.

Liberty Church now aims to befriend new people, to become a family bonded to each other and to God. We aren't after activity so much as attachment. The people come to us, we hope, not simply to be taught, but to be grafted into Christ, as our Revolutionary War officers somehow melted together under the Father of Our Country.

Our troubled hearts are crying for this connection. It is our fragmentation that is killing us . . . "the eye cannot say to the hand, I have no need of you; nor again the head to the feet, I have no need of you . . . now you are the body of Christ and individually members of it." (*See* 1 Corinthians 12:21 and Romans 12:5.)

In the end only His friendship can fulfill the yearning of our hearts. We're all really eating our hearts out for Him. There is a God-shaped vacuum in the breast of each of us, and we have to have Him "nearer than hands or feet." It took His bloodshed to accomplish the intimacy our alienation requires. I do not understand it. I cannot explain it. I only know that we are utterly alone and inconsolable except we somehow be transfused with the blood of the Lamb. It was not until poor lost Thomas finally plunged his hand into the gaping wound that he found what a friend he had in Jesus: "My Lord and my God."

8

*I Came That You
Might Have Life*

A prize compliment was given by a seasoned and perceptive maitre d' to two friends who frequented his restaurant: "You two always bring life to others." Of course, there is only one Lord of Life, but life is His chief feature. Our first chapter introduced the fantastic part Christ plays in re-creation, but here we want to notice what a red-blooded foe He is to pedantry and company, and how fulfilling to our hearts' desires. My father's favorite text appreciated Christ's employment: "I have come that they may have life, and that they may have it more abundantly" (John 10:10).

We won't believe it. The first word that comes to our minds when someone uses the word *sermon* is the word *long*. Instead of immediately thinking of Christ as the one-man life-squad who brought Lazarus back from the dead, and one day will all of us, we remember the dead silence in church, or the pall thrown over the proceedings when the minister walks in: "Watch your language, boys." We descend to thinking that the reason Jesus came was to shape us up. The "Holy Joe" voice is anything but lifelike. We say it backwards: "He is the God of the dead, not the God of the living." We have no trouble agreeing that "He is the way," and not too much with adding, "the truth," but we get nervous about recognizing Him to be "the life."

Life, with its exuberance, is so often suspect to careful Christians. One young minister in a far northern community was going to be late for church, and then in an inspiration strapped on his skates and made it just in time, much to the horror of some particular matrons who caught him bursting in. He defended himself: "I had to do it." But one of the wily matrons queried, "Yes, but did you enjoy it?"

A recent funeral brought home to me how far we've strayed from the life of Christ and rearranged ourselves under the glare of the law. A very successful businessman in his mid-thirties died in an automobile accident. His wife had coaxed him to our church twice, and he told her on one of those occasions, "If I have to go to church, this is as good as any." His death had occurred a few hours before dawn when he was returning from a bachelor party.

If this young man seemed to have some of the failings the church loves to condemn, it became immediately evident to me, when I was called out to his house at sunup that morning, that he also possessed some of the virtues the church has lost. For one thing, however good or bad he was, it was so obvious to me that he was full of life.

His lovely young widow met me at the door with her tiny two-year-old, clinging to her teddy bear and still in her pajamas, by her side. In the kitchen, visible to my left, was another attractive young woman with two striking-looking teenagers. She introduced herself to me saying, "I'm his ex," signifying she was his first wife. Her presence there so promptly, and the obvious love and respect that reigned between the two women, was only the beginning of the wonders that this man's funeral gave to us. The two women were close friends; they later joined the church together. They even stood in church one day and bore witness to the love and forgiveness that had reconciled them.

Their door was not only opened to me that morning, it was opened to God. It is always customary at a funeral for friends and neighbors to flood in, but I was thunderstruck by the swelling crowd that approached a thousand that sunny summer day. They were not there simply as representatives of businesses, or because of his success, but because of his vitality.

Several impressive young men stepped out of the crowd of mourners to introduce themselves as his best friend. "At least," as one of them said, "he was my best friend." One was a well-known surgeon, one was an architect, one a builder. One huge athlete came to my office just before the service to tell me, blinded by tears, "I don't know whether this helps you to know him better or not, but I want to tell you he was one hundred percent."

Usually at funerals mourners keep busy defending the goodness of the departed. I was struck by the way no one tried to whitewash this man. They were there out of love, because he was one of them. I never met anyone who actually seemed to have so many real friends, so many best friends. So-called good people do not usually break that many hearts when they go, for they were not that animated. Somehow this young man had escaped the pallor sometimes cast on church people. He may not have been as religious as he should, but he had also avoided the curse of becoming a dried arrangement. Something often seems to suck the life out of people stuck in the pews. This man reminded me of the rich young ruler whom Jesus "looking upon . . . loved . . ." (Mark 10:21).

Don't let your guilt trip, or your struggle to be good, diminish your vitality. Perhaps the priest who had as many requests to be best man as to be priest was a true servant of the Lord of Life. According to the disciple Jesus loved, Jesus was very much alive. Jesus' next escapade, after running away from home at twelve, was His flamboyant invasion of a wedding reception.

And He was not the rabbi solemnizing the ceremony. Jesus was busy that day, not tying tin cans on the cart, but making more wine for the festivities. Any way one computes the quantity, it turns out to be well over a hundred gallons.

Aside from this miracle at the wedding in Cana by this young man who, while He may not have been a spiritual Marco Polo, was also not a sickly wallflower; wine in Israel stood for "life." Along with bread, the staff of life, wine was the symbol He chose. He could have selected the Bible and the Cross, but no, being the Lord of Life, he selected a big night out to supper with some friends, who finally proved that they would do anything for Him. God have mercy on us if we've turned His generous bread and ample wine into a wordy, lifeless desert.

Instead of Jesus simply being introduced to the world during a judicious exposition of Scripture, or as John the Baptist was introduced, with a warning of "the wrath to come," Jesus performed His first miracle by providing the refreshment at a poor man's wedding. And what's more—and I hope I shall never recover from my astonishment at this—this was the very miracle that converted the disciples and made believers out of them. It says so in John 2:11: "This beginning of miracles did Jesus in Cana of Galilee, and manifested forth his glory, and his disciples believed on him" (KJV).

Not only John, but Mark's opening chapter too is remarkable for the impact of life. God's voice splits the sky at His baptism with the announcement of His Sonship and the descent of a dove. Then Jesus dramatically disappears for almost six weeks to fight off the doubt and the fear. As soon as He returns, He invites four of His old friends fishing for good. He did not invite them to pray, or sing Christmas carols, or copy old manuscripts, but to go fishing. In the next few verses He breaks up a church service to make a maniac sane, takes the fever away so Peter's mother-in-law can fix lunch, then successfully treats a mob of patients pounding on Peter's door.

Mark's fifth chapter offers even more incredible evidence of His passion for life; He healed one woman who had left a trail of blood for years, then went on to the resurrection of a little child. The Gospels present Him as no policeman, really not even as a teacher, but rather as an extremely athletic life giver. God's word to Adam was, "Multiply." Abraham's aged wife, Sarah, was not simply pregnant with a baby boy named laughter, or Isaac. She was mothering in him as many stars as were in the sky, including One in whom life burst forth so fruitfully that it gave Him away not only as the son of Abraham, but as the life giving Son of God.

Obviously most of the meetings we hold in His name are hardly jumping with life as was Cana or Easter. Liberty Church came close to life one Sunday morning after the sermon when the minister announced that a divorced couple very dear to the congregation were going to be remarried to each other all over again. There was applause. The minister added that everyone was invited. More applause. Then he said, "Come as you are. Now."

Then as a total surprise, to the strains of the wedding march, the bride shot down the aisle to join the groom who had somehow materialized up front. In a precious few minutes, using the old Anglican short service, the couple were wed once more: "Husband and wife in the name of God." Then the applause was thunderous, and almost every cheek was wet with joy. Couples stood with arms around each other, holding close. Some had come dressed as for a funeral, some to enjoy surreptitiously a little shut-eye: "Well, we better go since we missed the last two Sundays." But it turned out to be a wedding. That's Christianity. That's Cana. That's Easter isn't it? That's life.

I've never seen Liberty people any higher than they were after church that day. A glass of champagne never could have done it. I think it was the power of the presence of the Lord of Life.

One of the great servants of the Lord of Life in our time has been the late Corrie ten Boom. I agree with an admirer who called her "Corrie twenty Boom," for that Dutch spinster, along with her sister, Betsie, saved the day for so many Jews, rescuing them from Hitler through their underground. I still stand in amazement by the *Tramp For the Lord*, made by one old woman whom Christ brought to life in our time.

I quote an excerpt from that book because I believe it is the most remarkable of all of her remarkable experiences, and because, better than any other story I ever heard, it illustrates how the Lord of Life has a plan of life for every single one of us. It takes place during her travels following World War II.

Perhaps the greatest joy . . . happened one afternoon in Dr. Shepherd's hospital. I was allowed into a ward where polio patients were being treated. One room was filled with people in iron lungs. I had never seen the wheezing, gasping iron lungs before and they scared me. "Do you wish to talk to some of the patients?" a kind nurse asked.

I looked around and said, "No, I think I am unable to talk. I just want to go off somewhere and cry."

Always when I say that I am not able, I get the same answer from the Lord. He says, "I know you can't. I have known it already a long time. I am glad now you know it for yourself for now you can let Me do it." "All right, Lord, You do it," I said. . . .

Then I came to a man on a rocking bed. He had a different kind of polio and instead of being in a lung he was on a bed that rocked up and down. When his head was up he could breathe in. When his head was down he could breathe out. The nurse told me he was Jewish. "Ah," I said, "I am happy to meet one of God's chosen people. My father, my dear sister, and some others in my family died in prison for helping Jews. I too was in concentration camps because we loved the Jews. But tell me, do you know the Jew, Jesus, as your personal Messiah?"

The bed rocked up and down and he shook his head for he could not speak. He had a long tube in his nose and could only move one hand slightly to write tiny notes.

"Then is it all right if I tell you about Him?" I asked.

He picked up his stubby pencil and scribbled on a small notebook on the side of his moving bed. "I am ready to listen."

I stayed beside that rocking bed and told my Jewish friend about the great Messiah, the One whom the prophet called, "Wonderful, Counsellor, the mighty God, the everlasting Father, the Prince of Peace."

I finished speaking and from my bag took a small embroidery. On one side was stitched a beautiful crown. The other side was quite mixed up. "When I see you on this bed," I said, "not speaking, not moving, I think of this embroidery." I held up the back side of the embroidery. "Your life is like this. See how dark it is? See how the threads are knotted and tangled, mixed up? But when you turn it around then you can see that God is actually weaving a crown for your life. God has a plan for your life and He is working it out in beauty."

He picked up his pencil and wrote again: "Thanks, God. I am already seeing the beautiful side . . ."

The next day I returned to the polio ward and asked the nurse if I could speak with my Jewish friend.

"I am sorry," she said, "but your Jewish friend on the rocking bed is no longer with us. Just five minutes after you left he beckoned me to come to his side. There was a wonderful light shining in his eyes and he wrote on a little paper: 'For the first time I prayed in Jesus' name.' "

Be thou faithful unto death,
    and I will give thee a crown of life.

Revelation 2:10 KJV

9

The Trinity
Is a Conspiracy

Life is not popular. One would think that life is just what everyone is looking for. Not so. Life faces such strenuous opposition it has been forced to wage an underground war. God no sooner made the world than it was invaded by the dark lord. We can't agree on details, but Christians sense that all creation was involved in a huge tragedy. Whatever snake it was that bit Adam required God to become invisible.

This is no longer my Father's world—entirely. It is known as *Paradise Lost,* as Milton entitled his epic poem. Everyone knows something is wrong, and that whatever it is, earth is not the Garden of Eden anymore.

A conspiracy is a secret attempt to take over control. In a very real sense the Bible is the big detective story about God's recovery of His lost Kingdom. C. S. Lewis says in *Mere Christianity* (Macmillan, 1952):

> Enemy-occupied territory—that is what the world is. Christianity is the story of how the rightful King has landed in disguise, and is calling us all to take part in a great campaign of sabotage.

Scripture supports this view of God the Father and the Lord of Life, His Son, conducting a somewhat undercover operation through the invisible power of the Holy Ghost. In Genesis man not only covered himself, so did God. No one has seen Him since. Abraham only heard His voice, Moses only saw Him from behind. The Bible promises that the day will come when we shall "no longer see through a glass darkly but face to face" (*see* 1 Corinthians 13:12). But there is no way now that we can get into a receiving line and shake His hand.

One might have thought that the crossing of the Red Sea, or the presentation of the Commandments, might have called for God to stand up and be recognized. But no specimens of His handwriting exist. All evidence of His footprints in the sand have been carefully wiped or washed away.

No doubt God has many reasons why He permits no

photographs, but one reason is His engagement in this conspiracy to overthrow the opposition. Talk about the Mafia shadowing targets and secreting messages in restrooms; God made His initial contact with Moses in a burning bush. He approached Mother Mary and Joseph by angels and in dreams.

Then when Christmas came God sent His Son incognito. Not even Herod the king could lay a finger on Him. It took the neighboring shepherds by surprise. Immediately the plot thickened, and in a few hours, before an impending bloody massacre, a divine messenger succeeded in warning Joseph to hide Mary and the Baby Jesus swiftly down in Egypt 'til the horror of an aged king's death patrol had blown over.

Christ's coming was a cloak and dagger operation to the end. Except for that brief time He was a lost boy, Jesus dropped out of sight for twenty years, living in a place where no one would have suspected the King's Son to be. "Can anything good come out of Nazareth?" scorned Nathanael. And Jesus no sooner reappeared than He was locked in combat with the dark fiend for forty days and forty nights.

Don't think for a minute that the coming of the Messiah made everybody happy ever after. Even the brief flag-waving ceremony on Palm Sunday stirred up a storm of resentment. One would have thought, for instance, that Christ's raid on the graveyard to bring Lazarus back from the dead would certainly have had no negative repercussions. After all, who wouldn't drink of the fountain of youth if he knew where it was.

To the contrary, Lazarus' comeback was practically suicidal for Christ. Saint John wrote: "But the chief priests took counsel that they might also put Lazarus to death, because on account of him many of the Jews went away and believed in Jesus" (John 12:10,11). Contesting Christ was not over with this; the most sophisticated scholars dismiss Lazarus' recovery as psychosomatic. They get emotional about it. I know. I did it myself.

The tranquilized Sunday school picture of Jesus, with a lamb or a child in His lap, does not do justice to the menacing figures shadowing Him. Time after time Jesus narrowly escaped being stoned to death. Each parable He told seemed to sting some Pharisee to the quick. A miracle that would make one maniac sane, would drive the mob mad. There were people hanging around Him who took everything Jesus did as a personal insult, which is exactly the impression true Christians make on people filled with hatred here and now.

Every blow Christ made was a blow against death for everyone. Lazarus was only one, and Death didn't like it. The Lord of Life was forced to conduct a guerrilla campaign against this lord of death. Things Jesus said are capable of differing interpretations, signifying also that His mission was clandestine. For instance, when Jesus said, "Go and tell no one," it did not always mean modesty, it also meant that publicity could endanger Him.

Almost the whole world now knows about Christ.

The Cross was public. It has been shouted from the housetops. No one hides a light under a bushel. But there is so much about Christ, about the working of His Holy Spirit that one cannot prove. We have no signature, no album, and only the most dubious evidence of His shroud.

Christ's plans for the Last Supper were carefully guarded and under wraps. "So Jesus sent Peter and John, saying, go and prepare the passover for us. . . . Where will you have us prepare it? . . . Behold, when you have entered the city, a man carrying a jar of water will meet you; follow him . . ." (Luke 22:8–10). Our intelligence officers today incorporate similar covers.

The whole world united under the influence of an evil spell to remove Christ. It took the Romans and the Jews together to get Him on enough counts—blasphemer, disrupter, usurper. Judas was not the only disciple who deserted Him. Matthew says in 26:56: "Then all the disciples forsook him, and fled" (KJV). His conspiracy seemed, momentarily, to be completely crushed.

We believe that the rightful King has landed, but after all the glory of Easter, this campaign remained a conspiracy. We read that following the Resurrection even in the "upper room: the doors were locked." The 500 whom Paul says saw the risen Christ, even the 4,000 converted at Pentecost, were still only a corporal's guard against a hostile environment.

Lions dined on Christians under Rome's rule.

Christ's followers lived at unlisted addresses in cata-
combs and identified themselves with secret symbols.
Ichthus, the Greek word for fish, was used as an acros-
tic, by taking the first letter of each word in this abbre-
viated creed: "*Jesus Christ is God, Son, and Saviour.*"
No doubt a fish was often drawn in the sand, as it still
appears on ancient walls, to carry on the life of a secret
society.

Back in Roman times, as today in many parts of the
world, there were no church bells, or routine filling in
of blanks with your denomination. Even the word
Christian arose as a derisive nickname in Antioch (*see*
Acts 11:26). And those unorthodox and reckless ad-
venturers who went by that opprobrium, entered darkened doorways after the patrol had passed, blacked out
windows and preached in whispers. Books like Revelation are called apocalyptic and were written partly in
that style in order to speak in a code only the faithful
could decipher.

Now innumerable Christians are disguised behind
the Iron Curtain. The visible church is manipulated by
the Communists who appoint maneuverable puppets
as priests and patriarchs. So the true church has been
forced underground as under persecution in Roman
times. Bibles in any substantial number must be
smuggled, and any genuinely contagious witness
must be camouflaged.

Communists have no objection to a Bible remaining
on a lectern, and do not mind a few staged worship

services, so long as they reek with dust and death and don't exceed maximum seating quotas in those neglected ecclesiastical museums. I have learned this from my conversations with Alexander Ginzburg, and the heavy correspondence I have received from persecuted Christians in Russia. Facades are used as tourist traps for Western visitors: So long as God is presented as obsolete and no threat to their ideology, the Communists will tolerate it.

True believers must pretend to pretend to be Christian, or actually be Communists as many priests now are. One doctor who really was a devout Christian had to pretend to become a Communist so officials would let him practice in prisons, until he could locate his beloved pastor who was rotting somewhere in one of them. His uninformed fellow Christians suspected the doctor of working for the KGB, but he was actually a double agent for Jesus.

The Trinity must carry on its conspiracy even in our supposedly Christian country. Furthermore, the snake has not only crawled into the home of the brave and the land of the free, its contamination can be detected even in churches and church colleges. This is seen not only in their unwillingness to be amazed by grace, but more in their heartless indictment of any literary enthusiasm or exuberance. Hero worship and idealism is considered naive. College English departments wallow in despair, while churches remain preoccupied with the pedantic and petty affairs on the fringe of faith.

I see the ugly trail of the snake in the way many churches across the land seem to be half-dead, or half-hysterical. And the dead half condescends to the "hysterical half" as a naive anachronism, and the hysterical half looks down on the "dead half" as doomed and unsaved, joyless and lifeless. And people like myself presume they occupy a position above both from which to judge.

Victory for the conspiracy of the Trinity will require love for the other side, an appreciation of the other's virtues, and one's own defects, in short, humility. What is called for is a relaxation from this everlasting disparagement of others in religious journals, and in conversation. A moratorium is needed in this relentless effort to show up the other side, trying to pressure each other into our viewpoint, quarreling over whether the devil has a tail or two horns. So long as we don't love those who don't agree with us, we're being successfully ravaged by some scourge, for which we've got to accept, instead of shed, blame.

There are too many skeletons in the closets of many seminaries for them to say too much about New York, or for that matter, about Johannesburg. We are not to be afraid to "call" a bully on anything, but our righteous crusades must be chastened by a more brutal recognition of our own selfish and self-righteous hearts.

So the conspiracy of the Trinity is desperately needed in the most unsuspected inner sanctums all over this overshadowed planet. The holy of holies itself must be recaptured—I mean all the highly respected celebrity evangelists as well as country preachers—and very proper churches and spiritual underground renewal movements designed and dedicated to save the church. I mean you and me.

And the true Christian evangel must remain a conspiracy. We're not to the point of waving the flag in the public square yet. Sophomores would be better advised than to declare their faith too graphically by bumper stickers. Fellow conspirators, let us not all get into uniform, nor erect twelve-inch silver crosses on our automobile grills. "I love Jesus" shirts may not be the way to go in this country any more than in the Ukraine.

Carrying a Bible under one's arm, raising one's hands when singing songs with hallelujahs in them, or releasing doves when someone turns a certain phrase, may be appropriate on occasion. However, these differing varieties of "circumcision" are not mandatory. Since Paul removed the requirement of being circumcised, we should not impose new "circumcisions."

Jesus would shudder at some of the nonconspiratorial declarations disoriented believers make. Time after time He felt forced to rebuff loose lips: "Not everyone who says to me, 'Lord, Lord,' shall enter the Kingdom." We're not to pose as Christians so much as to try to get away with not getting credit for it. Again and again Jesus crushed the religious success story with comments like: "I tell you they have their reward" (Matthew 6:2,5). We're not to say we're one of His, so much as *be* one. "Greater love hath no man than this, that a man lay down his life for his friends" (John 15:13 KJV). We've not fulfilled such verses merely by memorizing them.

The balding man that winter night in the icy waters of the Potomac not so long ago when a jetliner went down, repeatedly gave his life preserver away until he disappeared beneath the water. Those of us in the talking business of Christianity must learn from him. He sent out no advance circulars of that courageous feat. So far as is known he didn't give out a text or sigh, "I hope you appreciate what I'm doing for you." He simply kept giving his life preserver to someone else until it was too late for him, because when the helicopter came back the cold had taken him down.

The word *witness* originally meant "martyr." We've cheapened the word considerably, but now and then, we find an uncanonized saint who does something so beautiful for us, after it's too late to offer him any thanks. Have you ever loved someone enough to listen to him talk, until he talked himself into Christ Jesus? We can't talk people into Christ. That's part of the conspiracy. Loving them, not loving our spiritual triumph, loving them enough to let God have them without our interruption.

"The Kingdom of Heaven is like leaven which a woman took and hid in three measures of dough until it was all leavened" (*see* Matthew 13:33). No one knows how or where. "Lo, here; lo, there." We are secure in the Good News, but in another sense, the Kingdom is "a whodunit." Sir John Seely ended *Ecce Homo* (Dutton, 1908), his unparalleled classic on the life of Christ, speaking of the coming of the New Jerusalem as though it were the conclusion to a cosmic conspiracy: "No man heard the clink of trowel or pickaxe; it descended (silently) out of Heaven from God."

10

The
Missing Keys

Christ gave the keys to this conspiracy to the church, and it has somehow misplaced them. While we are counting on its ultimate success, everybody knows what a blunt and broken instrument of grace the church has become.

Harry Emerson Fosdick loved to tell about the Church of God that split over a dispute. The faction that left called itself "The True Church of God." Then it too had a split and the next faction called itself "The Only True Church of God."

This is the sob story of Christianity. Saint Paul no sooner seeded the first tiny churches along the Mediterranean than they quickly fractured into conflicting cliques clinging to Cephas or Apollos. Finally, about a thousand years after Christ, the one true church cracked wide open between the Roman Catholic West beneath the pope, and the Eastern Orthodox under the patriarchs of Constantinople.

Five hundred years later, when the Protestant church was divorced from the Roman Catholic, it began shattering into hundreds of splinters, sects and denominations, all appreciative of their diverse heritages, but unrepentant for whatever shame had wrenched them from the True Church of God. Whatever became of the keys Christ gave Peter to the Kingdom? Unless the body of Christ gets together how can it lift a finger to help fit the jagged pieces of our world together?

The church is also called the Bride of Christ. Let me tell you how she may have run away, and how she may come back.

One of the great ministers of our city, Columbus, Ohio, shared with me his shocking introduction to the ministry. He was called to a well-situated downtown church that had remained small partly because of its rapid succession of short pastorates, none of which was over two or three years, and a number lasting only months.

One of the young minister's first recommendations to his official board was that he exchange pulpits with the black minister in the neighboring parish for Race Relations Sunday. This was during the forties when the issue generated sharp controversy. The chief elder of the board reacted: "Our church will not be exchanging pulpits with any black minister so long as I am alive." The young minister replied, "Well, we don't have to do it this year but I still think it is a good idea."

The young minister did not resent that reaction of that elder. He had a plan, illustrated by this parable. A merchant stood outside his display window chipping ice so as to expose his display to passersby. Someone suggested to the merchant that it would be far easier to turn up the heat inside and melt the ice instead. The young minister took this counsel for his ministry. He did not chip away at the chief elder's reaction. He warmed the heart inside by preaching the love of Christ.

The next year the minister repeated his proposal of the pulpit exchange and the elder gave the same negative reply. The minister in a good spirit continued to turn up the heat inside. The third year, to everyone's amazement, the chief elder himself brought up the idea of the pulpit exchange and moved that it be done.

The years stretched into the church's first long pastorate, and the young minister realized that for some mysterious reason he had not been asked to leave as had all his predecessors. The church grew large.

One day, years after the old elder had died, the minister received a request to come to the bedside of another dying elder. The sick man said:

Before I go I want to tell you the secret to
your long pastorate, for no one is left who re-
members except me. During your second
year the chief elder, who gave you difficulty
about the pulpit exchange, called a secret
meeting of the elders without you. Attendance was good, for everyone expected a
move to unseat you.

The chief elder called the meeting to order
and began: "Down the street is the large
Congregational Church. Its minister has
been there for twenty-five years. Up the
street in the other direction is the large Presbyterian Church, and its minister has been
there almost as long. Our little church has
never grown because of petty people like me
whose jealousy for control has never allowed
our ministers to stay long enough to do any
good."

The meeting took place in a little parlor off
the sanctuary. There was a small side table
with an open Bible on it. The chief elder
moved the table to the center of the room
and placed his hand on the Bible's open page
and continued: "The young minister we
have now is doing the best he can. Through
his preaching Christ has touched my heart.
And I vow before you tonight never again to
lay so much as a straw in his way. And I in-

vite the rest of you to join me." One by one
every elder present laid his hand on the
Bible. Then the chief elder made the prayer
that made your pastorate and this church.

It would be wrong, of course, to blame every chief
elder for everything that has gone wrong in the
church. The "keys" can be lost as easily by the minister or choir director. We are all at fault, really, for the
accumulation of grievances that keep feuds brewing
and factions stewing as illustrated in the church just
mentioned. But church leaders, as well as those sitting
listlessly in the front and back pews, desperately need
the amazing grace that happened to that old elder.
Until then, the Bride of Christ remains in harlotry as
the prophets accused Israel back in Old Testament
times.

What if churches nationally, as well as locally,
stopped pointing with pride to their divisive heritages
and began crying for shame because of all the things
they've done to each other? Did you ever hear of a
minister, or a congregation, or an entire denomination, apologizing publicly for its folly and failure to
present Christ? Did anyone ever say a convincing "I'm
sorry" for the thousands who've been martyred and
massacred in the name of Christ over the bloody centuries? What about the innocent witches who were
burned and drowned, the brave "heretics" who were
tortured on the rack?

And all that cruelty and ill will was simply a more

savage expression of the very same envy and cruelty flourishing in a modern elder's heart. When we stop to think of the religious wars, in communities across our land, we know that such sin prospers in our darkened hearts today as successfully, if not quite as physically, as in the ages we like to debunk as "dark."

We ministers and members have been so busy proving ourselves right and reproaching the world, we've left no room to admit our wrong. The time has come to laugh at the idea that there is no way like our way. We must laugh, and also cry, that we've been so blind to the showers of blessings pouring down on people who can't spell Presbyterian or who can't read the Bible and get away with it the way we do. Did we ever suspect there may be those better off without the burden of our sermons; that children might be safer without the sour or superficial spirit we inflict on them in our Sunday schools? That chief elder had taught Sunday school for years when his heart definitely did not belong to Jesus. I fear he is rather typical of many of us, or else Christ could long since have ushered in His Kingdom.

When you look around for good deeds today, don't assume they're more common in institutions we've dared to identify as churches. I see beautiful things for God being done with embarrassing frequency by those who were ineligible for our college religion courses, and by those who thought Luke was the hired hand in the musical *Oklahoma*. Recently someone laid down his life for someone else, with love and without fanfare; it couldn't have looked more like Christ, and yet this man had not been going to church, nor reading his Bible.

Our major denominations, as we saw earlier, instead of practicing forgiveness and martyrdom, are, as Jesus said about Martha: "Anxious and troubled about many things; one thing is needful" (Luke 10:41 RSV). The churches are dying; even devout C. S. Lewis insisted that we now live in a post-Christian era. Church business meetings bore everyone to death over trifles. It is as though we were shuffling deck chairs on the *Titanic*.

In Great Britain on any Sunday morning, far more tourists will be drifting through her majestic cathedrals than will be worshipping. The guide will point to a pitiful little sign which reads: PLEASE WHISPER, SERVICES IN PROGRESS. And huddled in a far front corner of the sanctuary a few veterans are roped off and staring listlessly.

And those of us who have fought our way out of the cold and cavernous cathedrals into what we like to call "live churches" find they have their dark side too. They may sing more singable songs and show more "glad to have you" backslapping warmth, but into this atmosphere sneaks an ugly presumption of superiority over other churches not so industrious. Bright-eyed ministers are usually tempted to condescend to other churches not gifted with the blessings they insist distinguish them.

The very fruits of the spirit have become footballs in a game to upstage others. We hang these fruits on ourselves, as ornaments are fastened to a chopped Christmas tree. They do not grow there in such a way that others pester us for them. The storefront church and the sawdust trail are as susceptible to pride as the very proper churches crowning Nob Hill. A truly joyful church will infect the church next door and the street it's on—not with a little "song and dance" but as an inner fire upon the earth.

Short of that sea change, "when the lamb will lie down with the lion and not be nervous," everybody will know that we mean business when we begin publishing, not the attendance, but the number of those who last week lovingly died for Christ.

There must be better ways of worship than sitting in one's pajamas and bathrobe in the church parking lot waiting to pick up the kids from Sunday school, but I know of something worse, and that is for that "parking lot parent" to get all dressed up and waltz inside thinking he's superior to any other fellows still dozing out in the parking lot. Whatever's wrong walked into church too. Not until the church somehow blesses folks outside in the lot will those inside have arrived.

Any time we try to tidy up our church dossier and promote what a neat church ours is we are no longer a church. Even the shadow of a church knows what it is not, knows it is not Jesus Christ. The church is lost that has lost the sense of shame, the sense that something terrible has gone wrong in the world for which it bears tearful responsibility.

Conscientious church membership-class leaders are so concerned that the candidates be informed about correct believing and proper pledging, making sure that newcomers are up to standard, but no one levels with them about what an appalling botch they as insiders are making of church. What makes us think we are members in good standing? Woody Allen quotes Groucho Marx saying something so true we have to take it comically: "I would not want to belong to any organization that would have me as a member." Perhaps there are at times good reasons for not joining the church. At least Abraham Lincoln thought so, and he never did.

It has almost always been this way. A century ago in this country, when the Bible Belt was big enough to cover us from head to toe, and Christians begged for two-hour sermons Sunday morning, noon, and night, many of those pious congregations were passionately involved in the most savage bloodbath of brother against brother that ever happened anywhere. Nearly three-quarters of a million American boys died in our War Between the States. General Robert E. Lee's wagon train of wounded, after only three days of Gettysburg, stretched out for seventeen miles.

Many of these boys were sent to the front from Christian homes in the heyday of "that old time religion," as B. J. Thomas sings, "back when people were getting saved." Christians were practically praying for

Christ to help them kill each other off. Christians? Not quite. Something went wrong in those churches. The keys to joy and peace had disappeared. And even non-members would know what a broken instrument the church was, what a far cry from Christ, and no nearer now.

No, it sometimes seems, as we have already noticed, that half the church is dead and the other half hysterical. The old guard wants to keep the roof on the way it's always been; the new life wants to wake the old place up. If only each side could see the humor in their inadequacy. The answer is not for one side to overwhelm the other; the answer is for the two sides to be reconciled, before we can ever be Christ's and help reconcile the world to itself. The answer is not to take sides, but to take both sides to heart.

What we're waiting for is a reserved Presbyterian who dares to open one eye to compliment an exuberant Pentecostal dancing down the aisle. We need a Pentecostal who will lovingly find a way to praise God that will be inoffensive to the traditionalist.

The Kingdom will come, not by winning assent for our viewpoint, but by our sacrificing something for someone else. We need to stop giving advice and to start eating our hats. We would not have a church if we purged it of those who can't see our point of view. A church is what comes into being when some preacher or chief elder takes some blame and shows honor to those not in his group.

I am not after a uniformity achieved by those tiresome political mergers accomplished legislatively at the expense of everything unique about our separate religious heritages. I am thinking of my dear friend, a devout Mother Superior in the Roman Church, who sighed to me: "When will we forget those musty old theological arguments and fall into each other's arms?" That is exactly why I think Malcolm Muggeridge recently joined the Catholic Church that Martin Luther left. It was not because others should, but that somehow each of us will be led along a path to love these "keys" back into the lock. And I mean by the keys that particular leaven that makes the church a colony of heaven on earth.

Why not pray with all our hearts that the members of the Body of Christ might sit down at His table again as did all the Twelve. He washed all their feet. Peter, who betrayed Him almost as badly as anybody; Thomas, who wouldn't believe; the Sons of Thunder, who wanted the best seats; Philip, who never paid attention; and Judas, whom we of all people should understand best, for we're so like him. All twelve were around that table in Holy Communion: "Drink of it, all of you." "I will not eat again until"—aren't *we* the ones postponing that huge "until"?

Not "until" the table's big enough to seat us all, until we're so homesick for those missing, those in the parking lot, those we've forgotten or rejected or who cannot bear our bigotry—not "until" then will Christ join us. The shepherd left the ninety-nine and searched for the one. How long? Until nightfall? No. Until when? He searched "diligently until he found it"—as we have seen happen so seldom to a self-righteous chief elder, preacher, atheist, communist, drug pusher.

Is there a church that might take the blame for being a lost sheep? Can we say we searched "diligently until we found it"? It was the late Cardinal John Wright who said, "Ninety-nine are not enough for God."

Will the church too have to die to live? Perhaps the church also has to go out and come in all over again. How can religious sharpies like us, who know all the key verses, and all the right prayers, ever overcome this immunity to the real thing? Do we need to take a break? Take a walk from the religious rat race and sit this one out, until He gets our attention? Then perhaps you and I can stop chipping ice and call a meeting of the elders that will be worth calling, that breaks through the bottleneck. And we be bathed in convincing grace.

We'll know the Kingdom is close by the arrival of joy in our hearts. The shepherd did not stop with the discovery of the lost. That's when joy descended. "Rejoice with me," He said, as the woman said with the recovery of the coin. And in neither case was it just a little joy: "Oh, isn't that nice." No, it was enormous joy, overwhelming joy, a Kingdom's worth of joy." "There is more joy in Heaven over one sinner who repents."

Mother Teresa does not simply do good to the poorest of the poor. She exudes joy. Charity can be such a lame and limpid business. "My father's business" is joy—not pretended, but planted, not boasted but harvested. Joy is like the wind that blew at Pentecost signaling the birthday of the church. The lost keys lie hidden somewhere in the field of joy.

I know we're in for a photo finish as the contest tightens between the two opposing forces. In many ways things will get worse, as they already have. But something remarkable will happen to sweeten and empower the Church. I believe that will be not when we see eye to eye, but when we walk arm in arm. As Reepicheep entered those deep waters, in C. S. Lewis' story, he could tell he neared the Utter East because the water tasted sweet.

As soon as Simon Peter announced that Jesus was the Christ, Christ declared that hell couldn't stop His church. And I believe He is already moving heaven and earth to dispel the mushroom cloud that's hanging over us. Finally Mother Church will come back to adopt this orphan world in an amazing flood of promised grace:

> And I will give unto thee the keys of the kingdom of heaven: and whatsoever thou shalt bind on earth shall be bound in heaven: and whatsoever thou shalt loose on earth shall be loosed in heaven.
>
> Matthew 16:19 KJV

11

Going
Fishing

Jesus' first four were fishermen. And when He called them that day He simply said: "Come after Me and I will make you become fishers of men" (Mark 1:17). Jesus had extraordinary style. He was not unimaginative, not all thumbs. Fishing further illustrates the artistry of His redeeming grace.

When the church lost the keys, they lost the knack for fishing. That wonderful sport of fishing in the hands of unsportsmanlike drudges has become joyless evangelism. That poor word has fallen heir to the most tortured abuse. Jesus cried out in horror when He saw what had happened to synagogue prospects: "Woe to you scribes and Pharisees, hypocrites! For you travel land and sea to win one proselyte, and when he is won, you make him twice as much a son of hell as yourselves" (Matthew 23:15).

I have never met anyone who believed those hard words were meant for him, but Keith Miller suggests, in his recent book *The Dream,* and I agree, that the church now, and clergy like me, need to admit that those words apply to us. Somehow we have ruined the fishing in these waters, or forgotten fishing and gone to meddling and dabbling; otherwise the spirit and the success of His whole conspiracy would be inspiring instead of languishing.

Jesus was sporting. Jesus didn't drag desks and swivel chairs to sit Peter and John down to business. He simply heightened their current job description: "What do you say we leave the minnows now and go after bigger fish?"

His fishing is big business, bigger than for profit, or for quantity. It's a quality operation. We are low-life creatures locked in a mortal sea. Jesus casts His lure to catch us up in a higher world. Remember how Jacob Marley moaned in hell? Scrooge tried to reassure him: "You were always a good man of business, Jacob." "No. Mankind was my business . . . the dealings of my trade were but a drop of water in the comprehensive ocean of my business."

Jesus calls us, not necessarily to Africa, probably not to quit the job we love, but to fill our own shoes. We are not only to deal with statistics but to pull each other out of the water and into the fresh air of His new world in order to inhabit that second life. We were born into one world, but we belong in another.

How beautiful of Christ that day on the beach to go *to* them, instead of sending *for* them. Christ didn't sit it out in heaven. He came all the way to earth. Then I suppose He could have headquartered at His carpenter's shop, and sent out invitations from there: "Dock your boat and come to my office." No, this landlubber went to sea for His friends. He did not try to take their world away from them, but He wanted them to have it hook, line, and sinker, and not be satisfied with a nibble. Christ forsook the security of His own specialty to appreciate life on the water where they were already at home, thoughtfully interpreting His ministry in their terms.

The fish became, as we have noticed, one of the symbols of Christ's conspiracy. It signified life in His new world; and it still stands for that first creed of His church, and finally forever, going fishing is what Christians do for the stranger and for each other; it defines the way, as well as the life.

We are not hunters, not bloodhounds, treeing people, despite Francis Thompson's "The Hound of Heaven." We're going fishing. It is assumed that a preacher should be a good talker, but to be a good fisherman we must be quiet, as we learned from Albert Schweitzer. And we are placing the bait in their world, not running people down. We're not scenting people out, we're coaxing them. We're not grimly stalking victims. We use a lure, and we wait quietly and provocatively. We are not in a hurry; we're going fishing.

Attempting to bring someone to Jesus by badgering him isn't characteristic of His artistry. Fishing is a beautiful way to save the world. We put the good news out, then we wait for the candidate to take the bait. Frightening people down the aisle does not reflect the Master's courtesy. He attracts them. It is our job to make the offer alluring, and to have faith.

Peter and John spread nets, a better image than the hook; they were pulling in the fish unharmed, no bloodshed, and so inclusive.

One cannot follow Jesus without fishing for others. True Christians inevitably attract a following. One cannot be filled with love and not act as a magnet. All the lonely people in that dark underworld are looking, really, for someone who can laugh a little, who have found something that steadies them. A godly person is like a tree, as Psalm One says: "Planted by the rivers of water that brings forth its fruit." It is the fruit that attracts passersby. Our fruit is our bait.

Christians talk about "witnessing" to others. Actually there is no way to avoid it. Everyone is witnessing constantly to his true self. It is not something one can turn on and off. Each of us sends out signals about where he really is. The perfect recitation of our memory verses won't screen our hostility. Our "witness" is getting across to the other person not in our words, but through our being. We can lay on another person the heaviest words in the world, it all depends on whether or not we're a heavyweight. The devil can quote Scripture, and the devil can simulate, but the devil can't love. He is faithless and filled with hate, and that is what he is really "witnessing."

As we have already mentioned, our loving someone, witnessing, means listening to them. The first thing to do with any drowning man is to get all the water out. Let the newborn baby scream as he emerges from the tiny amniotic sea at birth. Most converts have already been corrupted by listening to too many tapes from "witnesses" in love with the sound of their own voice. And our "fish" are desperately hoping, and needing, to run into someone who will put up with them until they beg to be loved into Christ by someone who has heard their complaint and been a comfort to them. This is the way to catch fish.

What's a good fisherman going to say when it is his turn? I think he's going to confess his own mess, in the style we earlier presented by Simon Peter. Just as Saint Paul on his way to Damascus to destroy Christ's company later inspired his audiences to Christ by frankly acknowledging his falling off his horse.

Judas repenting was no exception among the disciples. Didn't Thomas hang his head over his doubt? Weren't James and John ashamed for their mother's asking for the best seats for them? Philip was inattentive, and Nathanael faithless, and all were deserters in the end. The most effective come-on Christians have ever made has been to come clean first with their own failures.

Any fisherman is a different person after meeting Christ, but the biggest difference is in his fresh humility. We're accustomed to the reverse; of some mousy little person suddenly turning into "big stuff" upon his supposed conversion. Thank God, inferiority complexes are broken by Christ, but conversion takes place when someone's confidence in himself has been broken and replaced with confidence in Christ. Father Damien had neither credibility, nor rapport with the lepers whom he addressed, "You lepers." It was not until the day he saw the telltale whiteness on his hand, and finally greeted them, "We lepers," that he held them in the hollow of his hand, in his leprous hand. A good fisherman does not condescend.

The good fisherman also appreciates the fish. He's not looking for someone to work on, but someone to be with, someone to learn from, someone to look up to. He prizes his fish, more than his fishing ability.

Many fish are abused by their anglers. The minister may sink to looking for evangelical material instead of someone to befriend. A missionary for instance can stoop to collecting spiritual scalps rather than seeking to bless whomever God sends him. And the rest of us sit back, acting as if "What a wonderful place this world would be if everybody could be like me."

The true fisherman will appreciate his fish, as well

as the Bible. A recent film starred a strict orthodox rabbi going West in frontier days to serve a Jewish congregation in San Francisco. His most precious cargo, of course, were the scrolls of the law he carried with him. In order to make it across that lawless prairie he innocently teamed up with a bank robber. They became fast friends; although the tension mounted between the lawbreaker and the letter-perfect law-carrier rabbi, since he wouldn't budge an inch until sundown on the Sabbath, no matter how close the posse was. However, they helped each other across that wild and rugged West.

One day the rabbi realized he'd been taking better care of his precious bits of paper than he had his friend. Suddenly they were attacked, and a gunman was aiming at the rabbi's friend. Then the rabbi put down his scrolls and shot the gunman.

The Big Fisherman, we are told, cared more for his friends, than for his own life. And according to a legend Peter died on a cross upside down, for he felt he was not worthy to die right-side up like the Master Fisherman of us all.

I2

Interruptions
Incorporated

Life is a series of interruptions. We are in the middle of a good book or we have just sat down to dinner,
and the phone or the doorbell rings. Someone sighs,
"It never fails." The minister soars to the point of his
sermon and there goes the fire alarm, or we're interrupted fishing on vacation to take the dog to a strange
vet; then we have a coughing fit while we're changing
the flat. Making our way back from the makeshift
bathroom we fall in the mud; somehow our wallet slips
out, and, with night approaching, we are never able to
find where the day began.

Our tranquil prenatal life on water in the womb was
interrupted by birth. Death, too, is rather sudden and
insistent, usually catching us off guard with our boots

on, our calendar jammed, and our mouth full. God is absolutely dependable but completely unpredictable and so even this conspiratorial fishing mission is subject to harassments and elopements as long as we live; in fact this is partly the way He improvises His amazing grace.

Some of us, and something in all of us, cannot take interruptions, we want life by appointment. It's so much easier to live by the book. Folks can manage with things running smoothly on schedule, but they fall apart when they are busy running the vacuum cleaner and someone taps them on the shoulder; or the electric cord trips them as they turn a corner, particularly when they didn't get much sleep due to someone's snoring.

Interruptions do blow our cover. Detective films are forever using interruptions to show suspects up—whether or not they swear in German, for example. They show how quickly we panic, how long it takes to pull ourselves together out of shock. Interruptions tend to bring up whatever fear or resentment we've been holding back. A bride and groom need to know how each other act impromptu; so does the boss, before she hires her assistant, for life is really an inquiry into our capacity for being interrupted.

C. S. Lewis took interruptions and ran with them like this: "What one calls interruptions," he said, "are precisely one's real life—the life God is sending one day by day."

So Christianity is deeply concerned about handling

interruptions. The story Jesus told of the Good Samaritan hinges, not simply on his being "good," but on his being flexible. It was the early church, not Jesus, who supplied the adjective, *good;* we could just as well refer to the parable about the "man who didn't mind being interrupted." No doubt the priest who went by on the other side of the road from the man who fell among thieves was good at meetings, at the meeting he was going to in Jericho that day. He just wasn't good when things got in his way—which is what we mean by good. The Levite, too, may have had a good side to him that was timed to go off upon his arrival in town, but neither one were any good on a moment's notice. They weren't up to unexpected developments.

The Samaritan had that precious quality of goodness that came out whenever it was called for. The Samaritan was good for something out of sight, nondeductible. Gabriel Marcel said that love was being available. A man had been ditched on the road from Jerusalem to Jericho that day. And two impractical goodies, a priest and a Levite, were completely preoccupied. Only one man was free to help, and he was a despised Samaritan.

The remarkable virtue of the good Samaritan was that he was ready. He had the blessed power to improvise, that resourcefulness to imagine how to incorporate this interruption into the grand conspiracy. A delayed kindness may be a dead giveaway. The Samaritan thoughtfully poured oil and wine on the injured man's wounds, generously put him up in an inn—in the middle of everything else he had to do. Love is nothing, if it is not now.

That parable was Christ's fiction on an interruption; how did He do in real life? We discover it as soon as we turn to the Gospels. The New Testament is torn from His interruptions.

Jesus' famous nap was interrupted by a storm that threatened the boat. Peter's mother-in-law had her fever, and how many others sought treatment, on what was supposed to be his day off. Jesus was not safe from interruption even during His meetings. A maniac, or a man with a withered hand, would demand attention. On one occasion Jesus had no sooner started preaching when a paralytic was lowered at His feet.

Christ's services were seldom done "decently and in order" as we Presbyterians prefer. One time on the beach He had to preach from Peter's boat "lest they should throng him." "They could not so much as eat bread," Luke said. One time his family interfered. They waited outside and sent people barging in, to get him to quit and come home. It would have driven a high churchman crazy.

Perhaps the epic chapter on interruption is Mark's fifth. Jesus no sooner steps ashore, than He is charged by a raving madman. Then Jesus stampedes a drove of hogs over a cliff transporting that man's insanity. The hog keepers petition Him to interrupt His stay before they are plunged into worse trouble. So Jesus boards the boat and no sooner lands on the other side than there is Jairus, the president of the synagogue confronting Him with the emergency of his daughter's imminent death.

Jesus takes off with Jairus, bucking a tide of people. Suddenly someone grabs at His gown, and it is the woman who had been bleeding steadily for twelve years. As the woman is healed someone intervenes to announce that the little girl is already dead. However, as you remember, the Master of interruption is not distracted even by death itself, and after healing the woman, quickly interrupts the wailing crowd of mourners to bring the girl back to life.

The Last Supper was interrupted by Gethsemane, and His arrest. The Cross itself stands forever as the awful interruption to a young man's ministry. The Gospel was built from that biggest stop sign that Rome and Israel could spike together. He was interrupted in the act of death itself by the most callous catcalls and the spit and the offal thrown; and also by the thieves beside Him, one slinging insults, and the other requesting His final benediction.

How would you and I have handled such a last-minute crisis as came from the Cross beside Him: "Don't bother me now. Can't you see I'm busy dying?" But that's exactly when you always could bother Him. And how like Him it was to offer His final petitioner no postponed solution. As always, He summoned the last strength He had left, and poured it out: "Today." How prompt. How thoughtful. Tomorrow isn't much good to a man hanging on a cross. He can't wait much longer. "Today, you'll be with Me in Paradise."

"Beauty will save the world." Here is a sample of His artistry. He never promised unrealistic "pie in the sky." He brought paradise with Him and splashed it generously on every interruption, like the last huge stone thrown against His grave. He took it as an occasion to portray the immediate Glory of God.

This brings us now to the original interruption of B.C. by His advent. He banished night by the daybreak of the world. Three kings were distracted from their wars by a huge star. There were shepherds who permitted heaven to intrude upon their business hours. In the middle of the night they paid a visit on a teenage girl whom Gabriel had taken by surprise. Her fiancé, Joseph, had had the shock of his life by the news of her pregnancy. Then his plans to get rid of her were yanked out of his hands by the most overwhelming dreams introducing Someone whose interception is hailed annually in our most amazing day of all the year.

13.

Santa Is
an Associate

My credentials for speaking to you about this day, Christmas, come not only from my ordination to the ministry of the One whose birthday it is, but I just happen to be a nephew of Santa Claus. Since these are my first Christmases in all my life without her, and since she caught the yuletide spirit far beyond anyone I have ever heard of, and then to top being "Santa," became a saint in the homestretch of her eighty-six years, the least I can do is admit she made my day out of December 25. Some of you may remember that some precious memories of her also crept into my book *Before You Call, I Will Answer.*

If you had Saint Nick roosting in your family tree,

who made everybody else in the family look like tur-
keys, wouldn't you say grace for it the first Christmases you faced without him? I'm writing you about
my Aunt Alice for the first time since she died, so light-
ning won't strike me for ignoring a miracle that happened under the mistletoe.

My mother and father had lost three children before
I came, so Aunt Alice arranged to be present at my
birth to nurse me safely through that perilous first
night that had snatched away the lives of my brothers.
I was born on her birthday just before Christmas,
thanks as much to her as to my mother and father. She
saved my life twice during the holidays due to her new
findings as a graduate nurse of New York City Hospital; and due even more to her indomitable spirit that
would never say die when someone's life was hanging
by a thread.

I had the colic at birth and couldn't sleep and
couldn't keep anything down, couldn't get warm, except when lying upon her stomach. To have Santa
Claus come down the chimney was not enough. I
would never have made it if Santa had not come to
sleep with me.

The years went by before I saw Aunt Alice again,
but no day went by that she did not think of me. And
in all the accumulation of over a half-century of years
she never once forgot my birthday or my Christmas. I
have never known a Christmas or a birthday when
four or five of my best presents were not from her—

and they never once were late until her dying day.

I was a child of the Depression. My dad was a Methodist Circuit Rider, and I remember one year his salary was $300 plus a wheelbarrow of small potatoes. We would never have made it without Aunt Alice, who was by then the nurse companion to Madeline Dinsmore, the daughter of the founder of the American Express. While she lived in a fifty-five-room house on the Hudson and often wheeled Miss Dinsmore aboard John Astor's yacht at their own dock, no nurse got rich in those days; but since she scrimped, we got by.

She was how I got my first suit. It had two pairs of knickers, one for school and one for church. My favorite all-time gift was the red fire engine she gave me the year I was stuck in the second grade. It must have been a yard long, and I remember exactly where I parked it that first night, and I couldn't believe it was still there when I tore down the next morning. It had long white extension ladders that practically reached the ceiling.

My little sister and I started taking the sled down the lane to the mailbox every single day from December 15 on, and as sure as the sun shines and the rivers run, there waiting for us no later than the week before Christmas would be three or four huge crates. One would be oranges. Only God knew what else. Every package was neatly wrapped and tied proudly with never a touch of any kind of stickum, and in red ink, "Not To Be Opened Til December 25th," on pain of death. We never did, though we shook some. All were always signed so we could plainly see, "Heaps of Love, Santa."

The green sweater that I am wearing is one of fifty-seven she knit for me. I could always count on a sweater. If I laid them end to end, they'd reach part of the way to the moon. My daughter "borrowed" the dark blue arctic one I got my sophomore year in high school and took it to the University of Edinburgh to keep her warm. I guess it's still keeping her warm for I never got it back.

Aunt Alice did not just give you anything. She divined what you needed. The biggest gift she ever gave me was a church. Not every Santa could accomplish that, but one year on a sabbatical I was living in a cabin in the woods and unemployed. She belonged to Flagler Memorial Church in St. Augustine, and they were without a minister. She was doing her Christmas shopping early as usual, so she gave the pulpit committee the scrapbook she kept on me. Many dossiers of distinguished ministers were being considered, but none of them possessed so ingenuous a conspirator propagandizing and spying on site. The committee thought they were offering me the pulpit, but I knew better. Flagler Church pulpit was stuffed in my stocking with, "Heaps of Love, Santa."

I didn't get a sweater the last few Christmases, but Aunt Alice ended strong. Being eighty-six didn't stop her from another record-breaker. She insisted on riding up to Wooster to my sister's for New Year's with at least two or three presents for each grandniece and nephew in that large family. For the first time she was late. And that last Christmas got her down in the hospital for a few weeks, but she made it back to her apartment.

We honor, of course, the One who sent Santa down our chimney. I've known of ministers to toss Santa out of the church. They were mistaken. The only mistake is not to look behind and above him. Santa's a beautiful by-product of Bethlehem. You can see through Santa to the Star. I did.

Somehow Nicholas turned into a saint. That's what happened to Aunt Alice. No one but God knows who a Christian is and when it occurs, but I believe it happened to Aunt Alice in the last year of her life. I think she'd admit that her obstacle to God was her independence. She was the only one of five sisters who never married. She fought alone and lived alone all her life. This wasn't all bad. When she came North she insisted on her own apartment with no intention of retiring. She would sell only antique buttons. No sooner than arriving at our house, she fell and broke her good hip. A tragedy. She insisted on eating dinner but knew she must go to the emergency room immediately after. Remembering her always so straight and strong it broke my heart to see her bent down and now, something that could never be, the one who always nursed needed nursing.

She got through the first new hip but wondered why she was still bedridden. One day the surgeon told her that she'd never walk again without the other hip replacement, though it would be at some risk. I asked her. She nodded, "Of course."

She was slow recovering and then her mind began to drift, and she seemed to me to have deteriorated like most of the other senile incontinent cases living on purposelessly at St. Luke's Convalescent Center. Aunt Alice as I knew her was no more. Days dragged by. What to do? I believe God suggested this to me. I could not be God. I could not even be very good, but I could at least listen to this suggestion. See her every single day if only for twenty minutes, and repeat three things: "As soon as you can walk to the bathroom, we'll go home. I love you very much. See you tomorrow." Before long she began singing this song and dance with me, finally smiling. It went on for two months.

One day she began reading the Psalms even before her mind came back, and then the *Reader's Digest*. Soon she was her old self. No, she was not. Her independence had been broken. She was as clear as ever but clearly different. A spirit of thanksgiving that she had not shown before overcame her. Some enemy of hers would have said she used to be opinionated and prejudiced. But something happened to her heart.

She still couldn't stand and walk. She was flunking therapy. Then another miracle. The therapist happened to be an angel who divined what Aunt Alice wanted. The reason she couldn't stand was that the chair arms were too high for her to get leverage. She was put in a higher chair with lower arms and stood almost immediately. Each day she showed off to me, strutting her first few steps, learning to walk all over again. A wonder she had taken for granted. Me too.

Some of us are glib with our faith. We talk a good faith. Not that old New York aunt of mine. One day she said a mouthful for her. She said something she had never in all her life ever said before. She said, looking up, words I never thought to hear from her, "I asked God to help me," she paused and wept, then added, "and He did." Her infirmity was the card God played to bring her to the manger. She fell toward heaven.

The woman who could never be helped was helped. She went back to her apartment, lived alone again, and worked every single day unpacking trunks and packages. One trunk she unpacked had been packed fifty years before. Day after day she worked, sewing her antique buttons on cards to get ready for opening day. Her will was broken, not her spirit. She couldn't bend down and pick up anything by hand, but she learned to use a grabber, a pole with pincers on the end. Once she spilled her pills and instead of waiting for me she pinched up all fifty-six tiny heart pills by herself. She must have put in the afternoon doing it.

She didn't lose all her starch. One day she anticipated a long talk, and I explained I had to run. She exploded, "Well, that's what you do best." But then she asked me to forgive her, something she could never do before. She lived till eighty-six for a reason. It took that long for Santa to see where she was coming from.

On a June Sunday just before our trip to England, I knocked on her Delaware apartment door at 8:30 A.M. There she was just inside the door, leaning on her walker, with her coat on, hat slightly askew, punctual as ever, smiling and saying her usual, "Well, well, well."

She held my hand tightly the whole drive down the Olentangy River to church, repeating over and over, "It is such a beautiful drive." In the old Hall at 8:47 sitting in her usual seat to the left of the fireplace, she stared intently at the new hangings in honor of those who had gone on to see the full glory of God. Scott took her home that day. Katie held her hand through church. I kissed her good-bye in the churchyard.

I should have gone to see her that night but decided to phone her from Kennedy International just before embarking for England. I called her again and again Monday morning, but there was no answer. I called my secretary, Beth. She got my son John and then he answered my call at her apartment, "She's gone, Dad."

I'll always be indebted to my friend Vince for finding a last resting place for her in our little graveyard; to my son Dave for the epitaph, "She was a giver of gifts";

and to Sally for taping the service to include the pealing of the old bell as we carried her out the doors. She even left the tape on after the graveside benediction so I could hear ever so clear in the hush that follows prayer, the distinct sound of birdsong—which until I die will be my version of the music some shepherds heard one night in the heavens above their heads.

If you wonder where Santa lies, I'll tell you. She gave herself away and into the arms of God. I pray this gives you hope this Christmas as it gives me. Because the truth is, I didn't learn much about Christmas at seminary or from just anybody. If I know anything about Christmas it's because of Alice French Maxwell.

14

*All You Need's
a Mustard Seed*

Before examining a mustard seed of faith, let us remember those who have had mountains of faith. Some are listed in the eleventh chapter of Hebrews: By faith Moses split the Red Sea, Sarah got pregnant at ninety, and old Abraham, in the most astonishing feat of faith, offered up his only son so effectively that it turned that mountain site later into the city of Jerusalem. A shepherd boy leveled Goliath, other heroes were stoned and sawn in two for God's sake, and finally the faith of Isaiah pierced the B.C. gloom, and he perceived and announced, long centuries before, the incredible arrival of God's baby boy, which annually festives us like no other day.

The superstar of faith in the New Testament was an

officer in the Roman army. He came personally to pay Christ respect, and to beg Him to rescue his beloved slave from the door of death. Jesus, of course, readily agreed to go with him, but the officer said he didn't deserve such a visitor; besides it wasn't necessary for Jesus to go to that much bother: "Only say the word, and my servant shall be healed." This was the most amazing grace Christ ever inspired for He said: "Not in all Israel have I seen such faith."

One might think that Jesus expected such confidence. Not at all. He marveled at this centurion. Not even Israel, the inventor of this faith, had ever seen the like of it. Usually Christ astonished the people, but this time He was astounded. "Be it done, as you have said." And they found later that the slave recovered at that very time. (*See* Matthew 8:5–13.)

Titans of faith like that are rare but real in our time too. In addition to Solzhenitsyn and Mother Teresa there are unsung heroes around us whom we miss through our own lack of faith.

A giant of faith who comes to my mind is the author of those two prized books *Kidnapped* and *Treasure Island*. Robert Louis Stevenson wrote them under the constant threat of invalidism and the knell of an early death from tuberculosis. Another would have quit in despair. But the more difficulty heaped on him, the higher blazed his faith. Can you imagine anyone else saying, "I believe, and though I woke in hell would still believe"?

But sad to say most Christians are tempted to claim

more faith than they have. It is a common failing of
clergy to seem to agree to almost anything, to throw
heresy hunters off the track. "Do you hold to the
Westminster Confession, the ancient and recent
creeds and confessions of your denomination, perhaps
even all the words of Dionysius the Areopagite; do you
wholeheartedly embrace the particular doctrines of
Trinity and Atonement that church councils have officially specified from time to time?" "Oh, yes."

So many of us are tempted to profess like Jack
Crabbe, the colorful and rather checkered character in
the film *Little Big Man*. Wanting desperately to ingra-
tiate himself with the evangelist's lovely wife, when
she inquires if he is a true believer, Jack hastily responds: "Oh, yes, ma'am, I believe in Jesus and
Moses, and all them."

And of course the results of such sweeping gestures
of faith are not impressive. It is as though we have
hung ourselves on the reverse of Jesus' statement: "If
ye have faith like that mountain there, ye shall be able
to toss this mustard seed into the sea" (*see* Matthew
17:20). We act as though fantastic faith is elemental to
us, but we are betrayed by the molecules we end up
moving into the sea.

Isn't this the laugh we've made of His faith? We solemnly repeat the Lord's Prayer. "Thy Kingdom
come," but who really wants it? Isn't that why it hasn't
"come on earth, as it is in Heaven"? "Thy will be
done." We've said it a million times, but no sooner

step out of church and proceed to fulfill "*My* will be done in Heaven as on earth," for our idea is to carry on there, the scheme that we've got covering for us here. We glibly subscribe to this racket we've made of religion, while grim headlines swell up and the cause of Christ seems to be losing members and shrinking into footnotes.

We've noticed already how Jesus rebuked excessive praise, as in the woman who blessed the womb that bore Christ. But Jesus preferred those who "hear the Word of God and do it" to immodest pretensions of belief. "The bowl of cherries" philosophy of those who act as though they've been to heaven and back and life's a lark doesn't go over with our Gospel, which prefers obedience to boasts. Abraham Lincoln did not care for braggadocio, but recommended the wisdom of the hen who didn't cackle 'til after she laid the egg.

Jesus honored humility, not only in parables like the Pharisee and Publican, where He summarily dismissed the Pharisees' long pompous prayer and He commemorated the Publican, who prayed for mercy on his faithlessness as well as on his failure to perform. Jesus immediately took to the father of the epileptic boy when the father confessed, "I believe, help my unbelief!" (Mark 9:24).

Jesus didn't expect angelic faith from us any more than He wanted the foolishness of fanatics or the absolute certainty of the pathologically ill. Jesus obviously loved people to be realistic.

One of Christ's parables dealt with His dissatisfaction with "yes" men. A father asked his two sons to help him in his vineyard. The first promised he would, and never went. The second turned his father down, then later obeyed. It is a very pertinent and neglected parable.

The religious fast-talker, toting the eight-pound Bible and sporting the eight-foot bumper sticker, may not be the one who comes through for you late at night, as he crosses the bridge, and you are thrashing wildly about in the cold water below. It was not the vow that Jesus was after, but rather the keeping of it.

Jesus said: "If ye have faith so much as a mustard seed, which is the smallest of all seeds . . . you shall say to that mountain be moved into the middle of the sea, and it will do it" (*See* Matthew 17:20). It takes faith to believe that so little faith is needed.

Some years ago a student I knew taught me some of the meaning of this remarkable passage. He had a very young professor in beginning chemistry who headed up an enviable research project. Difficult as the course was, his students greatly admired the young genius for his unusual concern and compassion for them.

When it came time for their first test, the teacher was frank to confess: "Forty percent of you will not be with us after the exam because of the standards enforced by the department." My young friend knew that he himself would be in that 40 percent because he had gone over the material thoroughly several times and had come up with a page of key questions that he could not find the answers to anywhere in the sea of faces swimming by in that immense university. The teaching assistants appointed to help students were booked solid two weeks ahead in a vain effort to tutor a class of 400 students.

The student decided to drop the course rather than find out what he already knew. But he decided to inform the teacher personally of his decision, and to thank him. When he did the professor immediately responded: "I'll help you. You say when." "You don't understand. I have a page of questions." "Meet me at the hot-dog stand in twenty minutes." They ate and joked together, then went to the chalkboard in the empty lecture hall.

Three hours later, with the air and the young professor's hair filled with chalk dust, heartened as much as enlightened by that teacher, the boy broke through his deadlocked formulae.

Realizing what a "find" he had made, and how rare such a generous person is—even among religious people—the student found himself asking one far deeper question as he got ready to leave: "Are you a believer?" "You mean, do I believe that the Son of God came to earth, died, and rose again for us, so we could live forever?" "Yes, something like that." "No, I work with absolutes, and what you have asked is a variable."

The next day just before the exam, the student went up to the professor unable to resist one last question.

"If I promise never to pester you again, may I ask you one more personal question?" "Go ahead." "Do you remember my last question to you yesterday?" "Yes." The professor was standing by the blackboard. "Do you have just a drop of that faith I spoke to you about?" The lecture hall was empty. The professor looked away, turning the eraser in his hand. It suddenly got very heavy. No one before had ever exercised such artistry on the young professor. He was compelled for the first time to think this variable through. Finally he said, "Yes, I do. I don't think I could go on living unless I had a drop of that faith." And somehow a great load was lifted from that student and moved into the sea that day for that professor.

> "If ye had faith as a grain of
> mustard seed"

15.

Bright Shining
As the Sun

Earth is where everything dies and is reborn. Cynics say that nothing is certain but death and taxes, but long before taxes earth was already busy dying and being reborn. Despite those who insist that life always was, our planet itself is an eloquent demonstration of how we are born to die and rise again in a sensational sequence to the chapter on creation "with which we first begun."

Most of the inhabited earth is a graveyard every winter, which blossoms into a garden every summer. Each fall Jack Frost kills off the flowers and kisses the leaves good-bye. The birds fly off, water turns to stone, and gray clouds shroud the January sun. Finally, freezing winds burn the green grass brown and nature buries everything under a blanket as white as death.

A visitor from another planet during a February blizzard would never believe that purple crocuses will soon be poking their heads through the drifts. It even takes faith for earth's seasoned veterans to believe that the sun will remember to rejuvenate enough by May to melt a mountain of ice, making bald meadows sweat dandelions, and bring baby lambs running down her cheeks like tears of joy.

Our calendar is not an automatic cycle. It is a live lesson in re-creation. And life and death not only happen annually; every day dies every night. Grown men and women are lying down and passing out every twenty-four hours, "practicing dying by a little sleep," then coming to every morning, which is a preparation for something even more fantastic. Even the sun sets, then gets up, violets close and open in a miniature daily rehearsal of the annual theatre of the farmer shoveling dirt over the wheat each October; as the Scripture says: "Except a grain of wheat fall into the ground and die it cannot live" (*see* John 12:24). That's life. That's death, and life again. It's the way of all vegetables as well as all the days of our years.

It is also the way of all flesh. Death and resurrection are not only in nature. They are also in human nature. Rip van Winkle has nothing on a number of folks who were down and out for years, then rose from the dead. Gert Behanna, one of the most alive Christians of our time, was an alcoholic into her fifties. After her stupendous recovery, which was far more amazing than the mythical reveille of Rip van Winkle's, she began her famous address, "God Is Not Dead," to meetings of Alcoholics Anonymous: "Every chair here is occupied by a miracle." For her reborn listeners had been on their backs and landed on their feet again.

The father of the Prodigal celebrated his own son's return with the same words that could be said over so many: "This my son was dead and is alive again" (Luke 15:24). And this resurrection that we have seen with our own eyes in lives like Gert's is as amazing and as true to life as each morning's first light and April's remembering to come again after we're sure March blew her away forever.

Personal rebirth is as difficult for us to believe as for the visitor from the other planet. But this was the subject Jesus discussed that night with distinguished Nicodemus. And it wasn't about the rebirth of some drunk, which Nicodemus could grasp was needed. Jesus insisted on the rebirth of this very respectable Nicodemus. The third chapter of Saint John, as well as innumerable places elsewhere in the Gospels, is devoted to the necessity of the best of us being twice born.

Nicodemus's mother had every reason to be proud of him. His name meant victor. Nicodemus was an illustrious member of God's chosen people; someone presumed to be literally beyond spiritual improvement. Jesus floored him: "Except a man be born again, he cannot see the Kingdom of God" (John 3:3 KJV).

This is not any easier for me to take than it was for Nicodemus. I am not able to bear the insufferable way religious sects can sling this taunt in my face, to say nothing of those who fake it: "Have you been born again?" And there is nothing I can show you to prove rebirth in my own life. God knows I need it. But I would betray the Gospel if I didn't acknowledge how terribly crucial rebirth is for you and me, and it seems to me a necessary step to belief in the beyond.

A wife in a recent script described her previous husbands: "One was a drunk, one was a womanizer, one was a thief, and one thought he was the teacher's pet." It was not that she'd had bad luck. We're all like those guys, or worse, with the greed, vanity, or envy that we conveniently excuse and cleverly disguise. We all have some fatal flaw just as that woman's husbands. But she too was just as guilty, bringing out the worst in them, failing to forgive them enough to free them from their vice, blind to the log in her own eye. Her name is Nicodemia.

Every Nicodemus must be brave enough to admit that this metamorphosis hasn't yet happened to him, or else our effect would be more electric. And when it does happen to one, one is no longer so zealous to fix up others with Christ as to understand them and love them as is. We do not coach anyone into conversion.

185

We appreciate them into it in the same breath that brings us back to life too.

Perhaps the most dramatic examples of Christian rebirth occur today at the hands of that angel who can be found in the streets of Calcutta pouring out her life on those who've been abandoned to die. Mother Teresa never had a child, but by her love all these losers surely find out something about birth. At least the tiny ministry at her two hands as she kneels maternally beside their stricken forms provides the stage by which bystanders like myself, and that Indian monk formerly dedicated to the goddess of death, may come at last to understand the mystery of how "he who will lose his life for my sake shall find it" (*see* Matthew 16:25).

Life out of death. Astounding. Yet true to nature: "If winter comes can spring be far behind." Even Nicodemus, of all people, finally risked everything to stand up for Christ in the face of those plotting to crucify Him. And then that night after all was lost, according to Saint John, Nicodemus came to the Cross carrying one-hundred pounds of myrrh, and personally helped Joseph of Arimathea get the body down. Surely nothing short of another birthday could ever have borne very proper Nicodemus out there that night to the foot of the Cross.

The first light of morning, that even breaks into our darkened hearts, prepares us in the end to believe that it also dawns on us after death.

Easter, of course, is much more incredible to us than an Ohio Spring to an Eskimo, or even the conversion of an Ebenezer Scrooge to a Bob Cratchit. We can look at the graveyard and bring ourselves to believe that the forsythia there will bloom again in the spring. But Aunt Alice—and all those still lying there on the beach at Normandy, under long lines of cross after cross, each one reading: "Known only to God"? Will all these unknown soldiers and long-dead loved ones planted so securely, or scattered like seed to the winds, ever come up again as kernels of wheat?

Apparently our forefathers found this easier to believe. The frontiersman in Conrad Richter's *The Awakening Land* returns to his cabin in the Northwest Territory. His daughter meets him at the door with the news that his wife has just died and is still lying in the bed. They were waiting for him. He leans his rifle against the wall and sits down. Finally he says, "We'll bury her east of the cabin with her feet to the east, so when she sits up the sun'll be in her face on resurrection morning."

Are we too smart for such naiveté? Yet our skeptical age is starved for this forgotten faith of our fathers. Dr. John Dewey has long been recognized as one of the most distinguished architects of our secular system of public education. While Dewey's religious disbelief protected us from sectarianism, at the same time it helped take the nation out from under the God of the Mayflower Pilgrims, who "so loved the world that He sent His only Son, that whosoever believes in Him might not perish but have everlasting life" (*see* John 3:16).

A story is told about John Dewey near the end of his life that reveals the hunger of our best minds for the Hope of the world. When his wife died, it is said that Dewey went to a prominent minister in New York City to arrange for her funeral. The minister was understandably surprised: "Did I understand you to say your name was John Dewey?" "Yes, sir." "Well, Dr. Dewey, your reservations about the Christian belief are well-known. If I were to take part in your wife's services, I would certainly have to speak of the love of God and the resurrection of Jesus Christ from the dead." And John Dewey replied, "Sir, that is why I have come to you."

Somehow, the prospect of his own death had not changed Dewey's heart, but the death of his beloved wife had drawn him at last to the burning hope in all our hearts for that final birth to which we now turn.

The Gospels make sure we know that Christ was killed. Saint John won't talk about much else than Christ's last week, and the other three Gospels cover it in great detail. Jesus was all but beaten to death and buried by the obstacle course they took Him on before they hung Him up. We like to say, "It could be worse," but if it could, the Romans didn't know it, for they had spent centuries perfecting the most unbearable agony to horrify any foe of the Pax Romana.

Sometimes it is hard to believe that someone died.

Perhaps he drifted off in his sleep so peacefully one would never notice. They could tell Christ died. The seven last words they squeezed from Him stuck so deep in the throats of the Marys they're still there in ours. Friends prayed for Jesus to die that Friday afternoon. The Roman soldier's spear was overdue.

The bad thing about crucifixion is the struggle to breathe. The big Man had to pull Himself up on the spikes for each breath. The women must have gasped each breath along with Him. No doubt they knew immediately, as the intervals grew longer and longer between, when He finally pulled Himself up for that last time.

Then the relief, and the shame, and the utter finality must have leveled them and left them lying like corpses too in the relentless rain as the hill shook everybody else loose.

I see Mary Magdalene awakened where she fell by Joseph and Nicodemus coming to get Him down. No doubt she joined that ragged little procession to the grave.

Everything had happened so fast Mary may have spent the night retracing His steps. Perhaps grief drove her back to stand where He did before Pilate. Long after everyone had gone to bed, and the city was blacked out for the night, I see her going back to the garden and throwing herself down at the place where He lay praying, her hand against that same olive tree. Mary may have been the first to find and follow the trail He left with His blood, which came finally to be known and revered by millions through the ages as the stations of the cross.

Were splinters of the true Cross still stuck in her fingers from helping with His descent? Had she been the one to cover Him with a shroud; felt the boulder jar the ground as they leveled it into place—the last to leave?

How bright and brief the sun shown down on Him. How swift His summer fled; the clouds rolled in and winter fell. The worst winter there ever was. The day God's Son went out and even those who knew better couldn't believe would ever come back again.

At first light the third day, were Mary's eyes playing tricks on her? Had she gone mad from despair? The awful stone seemed moved out of position. She felt her way to the sepulcher. It was opened and emptied! He had been stolen! She ran for the disciples, then ran back into the gardener. "If you have taken my Lord away, please tell me where." But she wasn't speaking to any gardener. The voice said, "Mary." It wasn't just a voice, or a presence, but Someone she mustn't restrain—as real and recognizable as a rose in the snow. Suddenly it was April everywhere.

The disciples thought she was crazy. Thomas was buried so deep in the ice of disillusionment that nothing could ever make him believe anything else unless he could squeeze his hand into the mortal wound. Whatever it took, Jesus opened His wound for Thomas. Did Thomas hurry and wash off his hand, or never wash it again?

What will it take to resurrect us from our graves of disbelief? We can differ on so many beliefs. We don't have to agree on dating Genesis or on the date of His return. Martyrs have died for Christ whose position on Noah's ark was not too solid. But we can't concede Easter. That spring is necessary or there's nothing. The body of Christ really was stolen—by the "Thief in the night." No graveyard will be safe from Him. Some may seem to be able to get along without this hope for a while, but like John Dewey, none of us can ever willingly abandon our loved ones to the hands of any dead God.

The life to come is no shadow of earth. It's the other way around—we haven't seen anything yet, "Nor ear heard what He hath prepared." But being amazed by His grace here prepares us for the joy and "the peace that passeth all understanding" in that place "bright shining as the sun."

> *To an open house in the evening*
> *Home shall men come,*
> *To an older place than Eden*
> *And a taller town than Rome.*
> *To the end of the way of the wandering star,*
> *To the things that cannot be and that are,*
> *To the place where God was homeless*
> *And all men are at home.*
>
> "The House of Christmas"
> G. K. CHESTERTON